The value of a ki
curriculum: An essay collection

The value of a knowledge-rich curriculum: An essay collection

Ruth Ashbee, Jeremy Baker, Tom Bennett,
Christine Counsell, Tara Dodson, Kasia Glinka,
Harry Hudson, Jim Knight, Emma Lennard,
Jason Molloy, Ben Newmark, Naomi Pilling,
Rebecca Ryman, Clare Sealy, David Steiner,
Joshua Vallance, Dylan Wiliam

CIVITAS

First published
December 2025

© Civitas 2025

55 Tufton Street
London SW1P 3QL

Email: books@civitas.org.uk

ISBN: 978-1-912581-70-2

Typeset by Typetechnique

Printed in Great Britain
by 4edge Limited, Essex

Contents

Authors

Ruth Ashbee is a senior deputy headteacher and the author of *Curriculum: Theory, Culture and the Subject Specialisms* and *School Staff Culture: Knowledge-building, Reflection and Action.* Her work as an advocate of knowledge-rich and evidence-informed approaches in education includes working with organisations such as researchED, CogSciSci and the Confederation of School Trusts.

Jeremy Baker is Associate Vice Principal at St Thomas Aquinas Catholic School and an Evidence Lead in Education for Staffordshire Research School. With nearly 2 decades of senior leadership experience, he specialises in curriculum design, teaching and learning, and evidence-informed practice. He has led work embedding research into both curriculum design and professional development. His commitment to reflective pedagogy and school improvement has supported educators across the West Midlands in delivering impactful, research-driven teaching. His contributions continue to influence educational practice and policy at both local and regional levels.

Tom Bennett is the UK government's school 'Behaviour Ambassador', advising on behaviour policy, writing national behaviour guidance for all schools in England and running the Attendance and Behaviour Hubs. He has written seven books about teacher training, and in 2015 he was longlisted as one of the world's top teachers in the GEMS Education

Global Teacher Prize. In his capacity as Director of Tom Bennett Training, he has visited and worked with over 1,300 schools in 19 countries across the world. In 2013 he launched researchED, a grass-roots organisation that raises research literacy in education. It now holds events in 13 countries across 5 continents, generating discussion and change in schools throughout the world. A Teacher-Fellow of Corpus Christi College, University of Cambridge, in 2022 he was awarded an OBE by Queen Elizabeth II in her final New Year Honours list, for services to education.

Christine Counsell OBE is co-founder and director of Opening Worlds Ltd, resourcing curriculum for 300 primary schools. She is trustee of David Ross Education Trust, editor of *Teaching History* journal and series editor of the secondary textbook series *Changing Histories*. She previously led the History PGCE at the University of Cambridge, where she won the Pilkington Prize for outstanding teaching, before becoming Director of Education at the Inspiration Trust. She has wide international experience, most recently serving on the commission producing a knowledge-rich curriculum for Flanders. She currently chairs the taskforce overseeing Northern Ireland's curriculum reform. She is winner of the 2025 Medlicott Medal for services to history.

Tara Dodson is a parent, a primary school teacher with over 10 years' experience across all year groups in the primary age-range, and an educational author. In 2020, she took on the role of English Hub Lead for one of the Department for Education's English Hubs. She is a Series Editor for the phonics, spelling, foundation stage and fluency programme that she co-authored, and she writes other reading support materials. She is passionate about all children being given the access and opportunity to have a love of reading shared with them. She currently works with primary and secondary schools to ensure all children learn to read well. Nothing makes her prouder than 'Put that book down and eat your dinner' being one of her most used phrases at home!

Kasia Glinka is Associate Headteacher at Maplewell Hall School. She has a master's degree in SEND (special educational needs and disabilities) education and the National Professional Qualification for Headship (NPQH). She has extensive expertise in teaching, learning and curriculum leadership across both mainstream and specialist settings in Poland and the UK. Her leadership roles, including Head of Maths and Deputy Head, have focused on driving quality of education and whole-school improvement with measurable impact on student outcomes. She also works with local schools to strengthen SEND provision and delivers training on SEND education to PGCE students. Deeply committed to equity, she champions ambitious outcomes and equal opportunities for all learners, particularly those with SEND.

Harry Hudson is Head of History at the West London Free School in Hammersmith. He has written widely on education and is the author of *The A–Z of Early Career Teaching* (2025) and *Must do better: How to improve the image of teaching and why it matters* (2022). He is a regular contributor to *The Times*, Times Radio and LBC. He enjoys mentoring trainees and early career teachers, and has led training sessions around the UK. He lives in London, and enjoys choral singing and sport – with a particular interest in the fate and fortunes of Aston Villa.

Jim Knight is the Rt Hon. the Lord Knight of Weymouth. He works in education, digital technology and as a legislator. He is the non-executive chair of a number of education boards: E-ACT Multi Academy Trust, the Council of British International Schools, Century-Tech and STEM Learning Ltd. He also sits on the Pearson Qualifications Committee and provides advice to Nord Anglia Education, the Brookings Institution, GoodNotes, Edwin Group and EverFi. As a government minister and MP, his portfolios included rural affairs, schools, digital and employment. He was a member of Gordon Brown's Cabinet, before joining the House of Lords in 2010. He regularly speaks in the House of Lords on education and technology policy. He is also a member of the House of Lords Communications and Digital Committee.

Emma Lennard is a curriculum consultant, author and co-founder of the Primary Knowledge Curriculum (PKC) – part of the Knowledge Schools Trust – which is used by over 100,000 pupils internationally. She supports curriculum design and implementation at scale, delivering continuing professional development, audits, coaching and content creation. She has contributed to national policy through Department for Education consultations and she collaborates with organisations including Pearson, The Key and Developing Experts. An occasional speaker at researchED and the Festival of Education, she also trains PGCE students for United Learning. She believes curriculum is the engine of school improvement – when thoughtfully designed and well taught, it transforms outcomes for both teachers and children, offering opportunity for all.

Jim McConalogue PhD is the CEO of independent think tank Civitas and author of *The British Constitution Resettled: Parliamentary Sovereignty Before and After Brexit, Rebalancing the British Constitution: The future for human rights law* and *Unravelling the Covid State: From parliamentary democracy to the regulatory state?*

Jason Molloy is Head of Science at Saint Martin's Catholic Academy. He has been teaching for over 20 years and brings a wealth of experience to his leadership. He has overseen the development of a knowledge-rich curriculum that has transformed the science department, ensuring that students achieve strong outcomes through carefully sequenced content and high expectations. Under his guidance, the science team has built a culture where knowledge drives both academic success and personal confidence for students.

Ben Newmark is a history teacher, school leader, education consultant, school governor and parent. He has been working in education for more than 20 years.

Naomi Pilling is a curriculum adviser for the Primary Knowledge Curriculum (PKC), which provides curriculum resources, subject leader training and curriculum advice to more than 400 primary schools nationally and internationally. She developed and wrote the art curriculum for PKC while teaching art in various schools. She is currently writing a book for primary art and design leaders, which will be published by Bloomsbury Publishing in 2026 as part of their new 'How to Lead It' series. She has an academic background in art history and is also a practising artist with a particular interest in printmaking. She is passionate about teaching art and providing access to art for all, whatever their background or prior experience.

Rebecca Ryman is Assistant Headteacher for Quality of Education at Maplewell Hall School. Her career in education has spanned both mainstream and specialist settings, with roles including Head of English, A level English and Media Studies Lead, and whole-school literacy coordinator. She holds the National Professional Qualification for Senior

Leadership (NPQSL) and has professional interests in oracy, early reading and promoting academic equity for SEND (special educational needs and disabilities) learners. Passionate about genuinely inclusive practice, she is committed to raising aspirations and outcomes for all students through evidence-informed leadership.

Clare Sealy works as Head of Education Improvement for the States of Guernsey. Before that she was a primary headteacher for over 22 years in Tower Hamlets, East London. She writes about curriculum, assessment and pedagogy, and is a member of the Ofsted reference group for curriculum, teaching and assessment. She was also a member of the sector panel advising the Department for Education on the writing framework published in 2025. In 2018 she was one of *Tes magazine*'s 10 most influential people in the world of education and in 2022 she received an OBE for services to education.

David Steiner PhD is the Executive Director of the Johns Hopkins Institute for Education Policy and Professor of Education at Johns Hopkins University. He has previously served on the Maryland State Board of Education, as Commissioner of Education for New York State, as Dean at the Hunter College School of Education (CUNY) and as Director of Education at the National Endowment for the Arts. As New York State Commissioner, he secured funding for *EngageNY*, the USA's most consulted free online curriculum resource. He advises state education leaders, district superintendents, educational reform organisations and publishers. His most recent book, *A Nation at Thought: Restoring Wisdom in America's Schools*, was published in 2023.

Joshua Vallance is the Vice Principal – Academic at Trinity Academy, Brixton. He has oversight of curriculum, assessment, and teaching and learning. Prior to joining Trinity, he worked for 8 years at Oasis Community Learning as a school senior leader and as Trust History Lead. He has written extensively about curriculum design and leadership. He is an advocate of rich, narrative-driven texts sitting at the heart of history teaching, and has shared his own work on this. He has also spent time over the past 5 years speaking at conferences and sharing thoughts specific to whole-school curriculum leadership, and the challenges involved in doing this effectively.

Dylan Wiliam is Emeritus Professor of Educational Assessment at the UCL Institute of Education in London. In a varied career, he has taught in inner-city schools, directed a large-scale testing programme, served in a number of roles in university administration (including Dean of a School of Education) and pursued a research programme focused on supporting teachers to develop their use of assessment in support of learning. He now lives in Florida and works with teachers around the world on improving classroom practice.

Preface

Jim McConalogue

Knowledge has become something of a mainstay of England's education system, in contrast to its once much more highly contested standing within the schooling debate. The idea that knowledge matters is arguably now more accepted than it is rejected. Much debate about knowledge and the curriculum today instead centres more on the details, from extent to practical implementation.

Our aim with this essay collection, therefore, has been to bring together a range of experience in the discussion of a knowledge-rich curriculum, in order to showcase examples of practice, underlying inspiration and sources of debate. We wanted to harness the vibrancy of the many minds in education thinking about a knowledge-rich approach, to both move the discussion on and, crucially, to bring it to life.

As such, we have gathered the 'testimonies' of 17 professionals from within teaching, education leadership, policy and academia; professionals tasked with discussing the value of a knowledge-rich approach and how it translates into everyday school life, across both primary and secondary education. Our hope is that this set of essays presents an illustration of the essential features and promise of a knowledge-rich approach, whilst recognising and engaging with its potential vulnerabilities.

We are truly indebted to Loraine Lynch-Kelly, Director of The Knowledge Hub, for her guidance and powers of persuasion, as well as to our Civitas colleagues Anastasia de Waal, Claire Daley and Rachel Neal for their diligent editorial work, and to the collection's authors – Ruth Ashbee, Dylan Wiliam, Joshua Vallance, Jim Knight, Clare Sealy, Emma Lennard, Tara Dodson, Naomi Pilling, Ben Newmark, Jeremy Baker, Harry Hudson, Jason Molloy, Kasia Glinka, Rebecca Ryman, Tom Bennett, David Steiner and Christine Counsell – each of whom have brought great insight and skill to their contributions.

The aspiration is that this collection helps to articulate the potential of a knowledge-rich approach to a broad audience, in order to enhance understanding about the merits, debates, practices and realities of a knowledge-rich curriculum.

Defining a knowledge-rich curriculum

Ruth Ashbee

What is meant by a knowledge-rich curriculum? What is distinctive about it? What does a knowledge-rich approach look like in practice?

In this essay, I aim to give some insight into these questions. Writing from the perspective of a teacher, school leader and advocate of the knowledge-rich movement, I will share what I believe to be the key points of this approach.

The knowledge-rich curriculum movement has grown in England over recent years, gaining traction across all phases and subjects. While undoubtedly there have been some 'lethal mutations' and misapplications of the 'knowledge-rich' label, the quality of the core discourse has been remarkable, and a breath of fresh air to teachers who are now thinking deeply about their subjects again, often for the first time since they left university.

Because the nature of knowledge differs so much from subject to subject, the discourse among knowledge-rich advocates is often very specialised. However, there are a number of practical features that unite the approach of knowledge-rich practitioners, and these I will lay out below.

Ambition

Within the knowledge-rich approach, schools are unashamedly ambitious about what they want students to learn. They want students to develop expertise across a range of subject disciplines. For example, students studying knowledge-rich art at a primary level might learn about the proportions and basic shapes of the human body, enabling them to develop accuracy in figure drawing. Or in secondary geography, we might see students drawing on a range of quantitative and qualitative data to write about a chapter from Dipo Faloyin's *Africa Is Not A Country*,[1] to challenge lazy and ubiquitous stereotypes with facts and analysis.

The subject disciplines

A central feature of a knowledge-rich curriculum is the distinctive treatment of the subject disciplines. For example, to understand a human being through the lenses of science, art and religious studies is to do so from three very different perspectives. The knowledge-rich approach commits to teaching these differences carefully and meaningfully. Subjects are understood to have their own distinct identities, with different ways of working, different criteria for evaluation and different ways of structuring their content and knowledge. In a knowledge-rich curriculum we attend carefully to these differences and strive to reflect them in our materials and teaching.

Overviews

Curriculum overview documents in a knowledge-rich curriculum will frequently explicitly map the different types of knowledge found within the subject. For example, in history we will most likely see substantive knowledge (such as the chronology of historical events and the building up of substantive concepts, be they empire, monarchy, trade or revolution) as well as disciplinary knowledge (such as the knowledge of how historians work, researching the past and creating accounts and arguments). In music and art we might see practical, theoretical and historical strands, as students learn about how to handle a range of media; about the rules that govern the audio and visual worlds; about the analytical concepts that shed light on creativity; and about how artists throughout history have used these to respond to their context and their inner lives.

Design informed by knowledge

In creating a knowledge-rich curriculum, we must ask not only 'What is the ambitious expertise we want our students to leave us with?' but also 'What are the most effective steps to help our students to develop this expertise?'. This latter question informs the design of our curriculum. This is a huge task that involves us identifying the components of knowledge (that are so often invisible to us as experts teaching the content); sequencing these components to allow students to chart a meaningful course; crafting exquisite modelling (teacher demonstration); making use of text, image, metaphor, story and example to bring content to life; and creating careful sequences of practice questions and tasks to support our students to build expertise. Let us look at some of this in more detail.

Identification of components for composites

In a knowledge-rich curriculum, we recognise that sophisticated and challenging tasks and outputs, like writing an analysis of a play, solving a set of simultaneous equations, or creating a painting in the expressionist style, all draw on a number of components. Again, components that can be invisible to us as experts. The knowledge-rich approach commits to the identification of these components and the explicit teaching and practice of these individually, before students attempt the composite. Thus this will often entail students working on sentences rather than essays, short rather than extended questions, and individual techniques and skills rather than 'final pieces'. This is not to say that these larger, more complex and advanced tasks do not feature, because they very much do – indeed, it is reverence for these more significant undertakings that prompts us to see all the pieces that must be mastered in order to execute the whole with the finesse it deserves.

Sequencing and returning to knowledge, to build meaning and understanding

The order in which content is taught is of prime importance within the knowledge-rich approach, so that students are able to build on prior learning in order to learn new ambitious content. The intentional return to linked and prerequisite knowledge is key and it supports students to make links with learning that is already secured so that they can develop their understanding and expertise. Before studying the British Empire, for example, students of secondary history might be prompted to recall what they have learned previously about the Roman and Mughal Empires. A teacher using a knowledge-rich approach will shape this revisiting of past learning to highlight the things that will have most value for the topic of imminent study – such as military power, a ruling class, bureaucracy and trade.

Practice to ensure students think about the knowledge they are learning

Fundamental to a knowledge-rich approach is the understanding that students need to *practise using knowledge in order to learn it*. Learning is understood to be a change in long-term memory, and long-term memory is understood to be built and strengthened through repeated practice.[2] Students will therefore undertake extensive practice of the specific content being taught. The components outlined above, for example, would typically be practised in isolation before students are invited to bring them together within more complex tasks.

Scaffolded practice

In the designing of this practice, we are always asking 'How can we help students to practise so that they succeed in learning and remembering this challenging content?'. In maths lessons in both primary and secondary phases, example-problem pairs demonstrate a knowledge-rich approach. This involves students being shown an example of how to solve a problem, to then be given a similar problem displayed alongside it. Using the example visual reference, students can practise working with challenging content, building long-term memory and confidence. This then empowers them to go on to practise further similar questions *without* this 'scaffold'. As a further illustration, in a secondary English lesson, we might see students initially provided with a writing frame that structures the key features of an effective analysis of a poem. Students might use this writing frame to construct an analysis of one poem, before having it removed and undertaking an analysis of a second poem without the scaffold. Prior to undertaking this task, we would expect students to have already learned components such as key vocabulary, devices and context.

Sequencing of tasks

A key feature of both the above examples is the idea that the tasks we set students form a key part of the curriculum. Defining the granular detail of what our students will learn is crucial, but simply defining this will not help them to learn it. The brain needs practice in order to learn this content, and optimising the tasks for practice requires both careful isolation of the components and consideration of the best way to practise them. To return to a primary art lesson, we might see students being taught how to use their pencil for techniques such as hatching, stippling, scumbling and bracelet shading, and being taught the rules of light and shadow, before using these techniques and knowledge to add form to a line drawing. Likewise in a secondary science lesson, initially we might see students practising using the equations of motion in a simple numerical presentation, before they move on to worded questions of increasing difficulty.

Scholarly tasks

Within a knowledge-rich curriculum the unique natures of the subject disciplines are brought to bear in the format of both input (what we as teachers tell and show our students) and practice (the tasks the students undertake in order to learn this content). Tasks are chosen because they are optimised for learning the content in question, in order to build expertise in the subject's ways of working. Students in history lessons are learning history, so they are set tasks that involve reading, writing and discussing in scholarly ways, using the vocabulary and register of historians, or a 'proto-version' of this. They are *not* set tasks like 'Write a newspaper article about the Battle of Hastings' because this is not the sort of thing a historian does, nor does it support learning the components of what a historian does. What counts as a scholarly task of course varies with the subject – writing a newspaper article may well constitute valid practice in an English lesson. The unifying feature is that these tasks have been chosen because of their reflection of the subject or for building the components of the subject.

Scholarship

For many subjects, a knowledge-rich curriculum means the careful inclusion of scholarship – text or other material produced by experts in the field – to elevate the ambition of the curriculum, and often to reflect the contested nature of many fields, or the differing interpretations therein. As such, in history students might read and discuss text written by historians, explore different interpretations and pursue historical analysis into the same questions that are asked by real historians. In drama, students might study both work by great playwrights and performances by great actors, and engage in criticism alongside the work of established critics.

Why?

All the above is a significant outlay in terms of thinking and preparation for educators. So why do proponents of a knowledge-rich curriculum bother? The answer is multi-faceted. The argument most familiar to the public discourse within education is, of course, outcomes. Both research[3] and examples on the ground indicate that a knowledge-rich approach is most effective at supporting students to make good progress in their subjects and achieve success in their exams, thereby helping to open doors for further study, careers and financial stability that otherwise might remain closed.

However, importantly, proponents of the knowledge-rich approach believe that a rigorous education has value beyond the CV. If exams were abolished tomorrow, advocates would still believe in a knowledge-rich approach as the right thing to do in education. In a democracy, a key reason for this is the need for well-informed citizens who have the requisite knowledge for critical thinking to evaluate the claims of politicians, to read and understand analysis, and to be able to fully participate in society. When the prime minister talks of 'crossing the Rubicon', or party manifestos make competing promises over the energy crisis, for example, it is not right if only the elite can access this discourse. All children deserve a future in which they have a seat at this table.

There is also a further compelling driver for proponents of a knowledge-rich curriculum. We might call this a cultural or aesthetic argument. The subject disciplines, it is argued, are the heritage of the human race. On our little planet in the middle of space, conscious matter has been asking and answering questions for thousands of years, looking out into the universe, around at the mountains and seas, inwards into the soul. We humans have sought to understand what is around us. We have made beautiful things in art, music and dance; we have turned our ingenuity to shape our environment, using tools and materials to solve problems and improve our lives. Out of this asking and answering within different spheres, the subject specialisms were born. To see our planet's history in a jagged mountain range, to see the human reaction to the chaos of war in a De Stijl painting, to feel your heart break reading a poem, and to know that others too have felt this same beautiful, terrible pain – all this should belong to all our children. These are the riches that knowledge brings.

Knowledge-rich curricula: A key driver of equity in education

Dylan Wiliam

Over the past 25 years, a number of organisations, such as the Organisation for Economic Co-operation and Development (OECD), have argued that education systems need to focus on skills rather than content.[1] It is easy to see why such an argument is so attractive. If we focus on skills, then what we teach our pupils can be applied in a range of different contexts, including those that do not yet exist. In particular, the argument goes, if we equip our pupils with so-called transferable skills, such as communication, creativity, critical thinking and problem solving, they will be able to apply these skills anywhere.

Attempts to do this in the past, such as the thinking skills programmes that were popular in England 20 years ago,[2] failed to yield any significant benefits. In response, supporters of such programmes argued that the failures were caused by inadequate implementation, and if only the programmes had been implemented properly, they would have worked.

There is, certainly, an element of truth in such arguments – the implementation of educational innovations often falls short of what is planned – but the main reason that attempts to teach transferable skills have been unsuccessful is that they are based on models of human thinking that are inconsistent with what we know about how human minds work. In particular, our minds work as well as they do because they are huge stores of information.

As an example, get a pen or pencil and some paper, and copy the following set of characters:

ЖӘШІК

If you are like most people, it will have taken you something like six to ten glances at the characters to copy them. If you have studied a language that uses the Cyrillic script, like Russian or Bulgarian, then you would have been able to copy it more easily, although the second character might have caused you trouble (is it just a rotated 'e' or is it a mirror image?). If, on the other hand, you have studied the Kazakh language, you would recognise it immediately as the Kazakh word for 'box'. The reason that Kazakh readers can copy the characters after a single glance is not because they have superior visual memories, but because they are using their knowledge of the Kazakh language.

As another example, consider the following 11 digits: 02920344946 (it was actually the telephone number of the Cardiff office of the Curriculum and Assessment Authority for Wales). Most people would struggle to repeat back these 11 digits because very few people can hold 11 numbers in their head (being able to hold 11 numbers in your head at the same time was actually the world record up until 1980). However, if you know that 02920 is the dialling code for Cardiff, then all you have to remember are the last six digits, and the fact that it's a Cardiff number.

People living in Cardiff can reproduce the 11-digit string better than people who live in other parts of the world, not because they have better short-term memories, but because of what is in their long-term memories. The content of long-term memory is always and instantly influencing what we can do in our short-term memory.

As a final example, consider the following puzzle based on a segment in the TV programme 'Countdown'. The challenge is to make a target number (in this case 127) by adding, subtracting, multiplying, or dividing some or all of the numbers below:

Target: 127

25   3   1   9   4

Even if you didn't manage to solve the puzzle, it is likely – especially if you're familiar with the programme – that the fact that 25 times 4 is equal to 100 just popped into your head. You didn't need to go looking for it. The presence of 25 and 4 on the page, and the fact that you were trying to make a number that was somewhat above 100, caused the fact that 25 times 4 is equal to 100 to be instantly brought from your long-term memory into your consciousness. You may also have become aware that 9 times 3 is 27, in which case you have solved the puzzle.

These three examples reveal an important insight into the way that human minds work; namely, that it is the information that we have in long-term memory that determines what we can do. Some people say that it is not necessary to learn multiplication facts, provided that you understand the principles. For example, they say that if a pupil does not know what 6 times 6 is, but knows that 3 times 6 is 18 and can double this to get 36, then that's OK, but it really isn't. The child who needs to work out what 6 times 6 is by doubling 18 has used valuable working memory space to do this, whereas the child who knows that 6 times 6 is 36 has already moved on.

This is important because working memory is limited in duration; without refreshing it by repeating things to ourselves, it is gone in about 20 seconds. It is also limited in capacity. While the exact number of things we can hold in our working memory at the same time varies from person to person, and depends on exactly what we are holding in memory, most people can only hold around four to seven things in their working memory at the same time. And while the capacity of working memory increases naturally as children reach adolescence, literally hundreds of attempts have shown that working memory cannot be increased.[3] The way we make our children smarter is not by giving them practice in thinking. We need to give them more to think *with*. We make our pupils smarter by increasing the knowledge they have in their heads.

This is true even for so-called '21st century skills' like critical thinking. When people talk about critical thinking, it sounds like they are talking about a single thing. If you ask history teachers and mathematics teachers to describe what they mean by 'critical thinking' they say very similar things, so it is not surprising that many people think it's a single complex skill. However, no amount of training pupils to think critically in history has any impact on their ability to think critically in mathematics. Critical thinking is a bundle of superficially similar skills that rely on fundamentally different cognitive processes.

The same thing is true of creativity. People often claim that young children are more creative than adults, and if you use tests of creativity such as the widely used Torrance Tests of Creative Thinking,[4] for example by asking pupils for uses of a tin can, then young children do come up with more ideas than adults. However, the most widely accepted definition of creativity is having novel ideas *that have value*, and the second part of the definition is often ignored. Blowing through the wrong end of a trumpet is not creative. The playing of Miles Davis is. Someone once described creativity as making novel selections from well-stocked shelves, and that is why creativity requires having a lot of knowledge about the field in which one wants to be creative.

Knowledge is also important in fundamental processes like reading comprehension. All teachers are, or at least should be, concerned with developing their pupils' ability to comprehend what they are reading. However, this too is often treated like a generic skill, where teachers try to help pupils 'get the main idea of the paragraph', but the ability to convert letters into sounds can only take you so far. Beyond the earliest stages, progress in reading requires background knowledge, as has been demonstrated in a number of studies.

For example, in a German study, third-, fifth- and seventh-grade pupils heard (twice) and read a story about a young player's experiences during a football game, and were tested on their recall of the content of the story 15 minutes later.[5] As might be expected, pupils with a good knowledge of football and good reading skills scored highest, averaging 17 out of 20. What was less obvious is that those with poor reading skills but a good knowledge of football averaged 16, while those with a limited understanding of football, whether they were fluent readers or not, averaged just 11 out of 20.

Even when readers can make sense of a passage, if they lack background knowledge they may not make the right sense of it, as E. D. Hirsch, the driving force behind the Core Knowledge Foundation, points out by showing American readers a paragraph from an account of a cricket match in *The Guardian* newspaper:

> Thus, as the final day dawned and a near capacity crowd lustily cheered every run Australia mustered, much depended on Ponting and the new wizard of Oz, Mike Hussey, the two overnight batsmen. But this duo perished either side of lunch

– the latter a little unfortunate to be adjudged leg-before –
and with Andrew Symonds, too, being shown the dreaded
finger off an inside edge, the inevitable beckoned, bar the
pyrotechnics of Michael Clarke and the ninth wicket.[6]

American readers would struggle to make sense of this,
not because they are unfamiliar with the words used, but
because they lack the background knowledge to understand
what the paragraph is describing. More importantly,
American readers, unfamiliar with the way that cricket
umpires indicate that a batsman is out, would not realise
that 'the dreaded finger' is, in fact, the index finger. A lack
of background knowledge makes it hard to make sense of
what one is reading, but often also means that the sense that
one does make is not, in fact, correct. The key to becoming a
better reader is to read widely, across all school subjects, and
that is why a balanced and broadly based education – one
that systematically builds pupils' knowledge across a range
of subjects – is essential.

Systematically building pupils' background knowledge
is also essential for equity. When the education systems
of France and Sweden moved away from systematically
building knowledge and focused more on generic skills,
the gap in achievement between those from more affluent
and less affluent homes increased, for the simple reason that
the children in the more affluent homes were acquiring the
necessary background knowledge at home.[7]

Now this is not to say that this is the only thing we should
be doing in schools. We need to help our pupils to become
confident, resilient, curious learners. We know that pupils
often prefer approaches to study that are less effective.[8] We
need our pupils to understand that effective learning often
feels uncomfortable, and to choose approaches to study that
are effective.[9]

Perhaps the most important take-away here is that the debate over 'skills versus content' dissolves once we recognise that knowledge is the pre-condition for every higher-order skill we value. Whether a pupil is solving algebraic equations, analysing a poem, or designing a solar car, her or his working memory can only operate on the facts and concepts stored in their long-term memory. Attempts to shortcut this – by teaching generic 'critical thinking' or 'creativity' in a vacuum – merely privilege those who are acquiring this knowledge at home. A *knowledge-rich curriculum* systematically builds for all pupils the background information that affluent pupils may acquire incidentally, giving every learner the intellectual capital needed to read deeply, reason flexibly and create authentically. This is not to deny the importance of curiosity, resilience, or problem solving; rather, it is to locate their engine. When pupils possess a broad, secure knowledge base, struggle becomes productive instead of paralysing, and creativity becomes the art of making novel selections from those well-stocked shelves, not rummaging for missing parts. Our task as educators is clear: curate coherent, cumulative bodies of knowledge across the whole curriculum, teach them with high expectations and effective pedagogy, and trust that the skills debate will take care of itself – because skills flourish most where knowledge is abundant.

Why not everyone has been convinced about the benefits of a knowledge-rich curriculum

Joshua Vallance

One of the things I say a lot at school is 'What's the 2 per cent of truth in it?'. To a student upset about being given a detention, in our senior leadership team meetings, in frank conversations with my principal – what's the 2 per cent of truth in it? It's pretty disarming and allows for a moment of sincere reflection. Perhaps it even allows for someone to say 'I got it wrong'.

I'm an advocate of knowledge-rich curricula. Though I came into teaching in 2016 when they were well underway, I've always understood the Michael Gove/Nick Gibb reforms. I think the Ofsted education inspection framework produced under the previous government makes sense and puts the emphasis on the right thing – the curriculum.[1] As a school leader, I've found the research review series[2] to be vital in shaping my understanding of knowledge and curriculum outside my own subject, history.

The argument that a knowledge-rich curriculum doesn't provide children with the requisite skills to navigate the modern, digital age has never made sense to me. It seems pretty clear, for instance, that someone thinking critically would be doing so on a foundation of domain-specific knowledge. Experts in their field are able to think critically because they are precisely that – experts. They can draw on vast networks of interconnected knowledge and piece together creative solutions. The skills themselves cannot be divorced from this knowledge.

And yet, while it feels clear to me, there are clearly some (many?) who are yet to be convinced. The arguments against a knowledge-rich approach are many and varied, and go well beyond the above reasoning around skills in the digital age. Some deal with implementation failures while others dispute the validity and usefulness of the term 'knowledge rich' itself. Some come from teachers, some from policymakers and others from academics.

The questions that we (i.e. those who have long advocated a knowledge-rich approach to curriculum) must confront are: what's the 2 per cent of truth in what they're saying? Where is the validity in their argument? Where are the uncomfortable truths about what has not gone well? Where might we – knowledge-rich curriculum advocates – pause, reflect and admit we were wrong? In answering these questions, I believe that we can arrive at a point of healthy reflection and chart a course forward, together.

In order to do this, it's worth looking back and considering what the so-called 'knowledge turn' was trying to achieve. The reforms to education policy that began in 2010 aimed to create a tougher, more traditional, knowledge-based system that raised expectations for all students, especially the disadvantaged. The intellectual heft behind such a transition came in two forms. First, in 2015 schools minister Nick Gibb wrote an essay entitled 'How E. D. Hirsch Came to Shape UK Government Policy'.[3] E. D. Hirsch's core belief was that for children to be truly culturally literate, they had to master a shared foundation of core knowledge: a specific, sequenced body of facts.[4]

The second influence was less overt, but no less significant. Speaking at the researchED National Conference in 2018,

Nick Gibb noted that a 'knowledge-rich approach guided our reform of all the subjects in the National Curriculum in 2014'.[5] Within the same speech, Nick Gibb also noted that it is 'incumbent upon schools to ensure children are endowed with the powerful knowledge' which, he argued, equips students to 'approach problems as experts'. The term 'powerful knowledge' appeared again in 2019 in relation to the new draft Ofsted framework. Speaking at the Wonder Years curriculum conference, then Ofsted chief Amanda Spielman reiterated the need to 'see pupils being taught powerful knowledge'.[6]

Clearly, then, the concept of powerful knowledge featured in the minds of policymakers (enough, at least, to draw comment from the co-originator of the term, sociologist Michael Young).[7] And while this is *not* an essay on the concept of powerful knowledge and the extent to which this influenced those in power, it *is* an interrogation of common criticisms of the knowledge 'turn'. To meaningfully engage with these criticisms, it's vital to understand the concept of powerful knowledge and its place within policy discourse.

In Michael Young *et al*'s work, *Knowledge and the Future School*, powerful knowledge is defined as knowledge that takes children beyond their lived experiences.[8] The argument is one of entitlement. In essence, 'the curriculum should be based first and foremost on the knowledge we consider all young people should have access to and begin to acquire during their school years'.[9]

Within their work, Michael Young *et al* point towards Michael Young and Johan Muller's three educational 'futures':

1. The Future 1 vision is deeply traditional. In this scenario, the 'knowledge of the powerful' is fixed and transmitted via classical school subjects.

2. Future 2 is set up as a response to Future 1. In Future 2, the centrality of knowledge is broadly rejected in favour of transferrable skills.

3. In Future 3, the term 'powerful knowledge' is used to describe knowledge that has been tested, formed and challenged by society. Powerful knowledge exists in specialised communities and is open to critique by scholars, academics and other members of society. Powerful knowledge is not fixed, but is not elusive either. It is a way of seeing knowledge in terms of its creation and purpose.[10,11]

In referencing powerful knowledge in official discourse, we can take it that a Future 3 scenario was at least part of the vision for both the 2014 national curriculum and the 2019 Ofsted framework. A vision in which dynamic discussions around knowledge and the curriculum would take centre stage in school departments, and where students would access not only a central core body of knowledge but would also be inducted into the distinctive disciplinary 'codes' of their subjects. A vision for curricula that was both rigorous and dynamic: knowledge rich.

And yet, when surveying the current landscape in schools, the picture is murkier. You will visit some schools where a knowledge-rich curriculum means rote learning from knowledge organisers (concise summaries of key facts about a topic). In others, retrieval practice takes place every 20 minutes as children desperately repeat a process of memorisation and repetition of substantive knowledge.

The criticism that targets the approach taken by these schools is that knowledge-rich curricula stifle joy and creativity, and rob children of the joy of learning. At the extreme end are those critics who cite the work of philosopher and educator Paulo Freire, such as his book *Pedagogy of the Oppressed*.[12] Within this critique, the issue with knowledge-rich curricula is that children are rendered passive. Learning becomes the act of 'depositing' information.[13]

This version of a knowledge-rich curriculum is of course a long way off the vision painted by advocate policymakers and Ofsted. And, whether the portrayal is a caricature or not, the reality is that some (again, many?) believe that this is what the knowledge turn is all about. This portrayal envisages children as empty vessels being pumped with knowledge that is to be memorised and regurgitated for the purpose of exam success. Within this, children are unchanged by their encounter with new knowledge and are certainly unaware of the purpose of this knowledge. More Future 1 than Future 3.

There is, unfortunately, merit in this criticism. It *is* the case that the attempted implementation of knowledge-rich principles into some school curricula has been poor. It *is* true that some multi-academy trusts impose the use of poorly designed centralised curricula across their schools. And it *is* the case that in some environments the principles of cognitive science have led to problematically generic pedagogies and the distortion of subject specificity. In these cases, something deeper has also happened. The relationship between the teacher and the curriculum, and therefore the teacher and their student, has changed. The curriculum has become something that is 'done to' teachers and not 'done *with*' them. With teachers – and in many instances heads of department – being stripped of autonomy, their engagement in the substance of the curriculum inevitably wanes. Teachers impart knowledge that they themselves haven't had a hand in curating, and children passively receive this in the name of cognitive science.

The 2 per cent of truth, therefore, is that this is what a knowledge-rich curriculum has become in some schools and for some teachers. A distortion? Yes. The intention? Of course not. But the reality? Absolutely. So how have we got here?

In some ways, this disastrous outcome is one of our own making. There is, undeniably, a conceptual vagueness to the term 'knowledge rich'. When defining it, people often defer to what it is *not* instead of what it is. Amongst policymakers, the term has been used extensively.[14] In his 2021 address to a Social Market Foundation panel, Nick Gibb related the term 'knowledge rich' to a 'moral duty to teach them [young people] important facts and truths'.[15] In Ofsted's 2019 overview of the research underpinning their inspection framework, they noted that 'In knowledge-rich schools, the leaders see the curriculum as the mastery of a body of subject-specific knowledge defined by the school.'[16]

And yet, for a term that is regularly cited by policymakers, used widely in schools, features heavily in education discourse and appears in Ofsted reports,[17] 'knowledge rich' is remarkably ill-defined. In the introduction to *What Should Schools Teach?*, Alka Sehgal Cuthbert and Alex Standish rightly point out that there is little clarity in the Ofsted 2019 research framework around the terms 'knowledge-led', 'knowledge-engaged' and 'skills-led'.[18] Without meaningful characterisations of these terms, school leaders and teachers are left looking for answers elsewhere. The term 'knowledge rich' therefore increasingly falls open to interpretation, and the lethal mutations begin to occur.

Beyond definitions, there is also the issue of resourcing. Curriculum work is hard. In fact, it is likely the most intellectually challenging work that teachers will have done since their own university degrees. Conceptualising terms like 'substantive' and 'disciplinary' knowledge can take time. Understanding that knowledge is not fixed, and that disciplinary elements of knowledge should feature in school curricula is not a straightforward task. Let alone for someone teaching 20 to 24 lessons a week.

This, in conjunction with the inevitable pressures placed on teachers by senior leaders desperate to satisfy Ofsted's demands (or, at least, their interpretation of these) has also contributed to pockets of poor implementation. In these scenarios, we see school curricula reduced to knowledge organisers and memorisation, the rote learning of canonical knowledge, and endless hours spent on retrieval.

To be clear, I do not think that schools and teachers are to blame for this. Realising exceptional curricula across all subjects in a school, to fulfil the ideals of Michael Young and Johan Muller's Future 3, is, by definition, exceptional. There are very few places where this has happened. Where it has, behaviour is often exceptional, experienced teachers are given time to work with colleagues to wrestle with subject-specific curriculum problems, strong subject communities exist, leadership is stable, teaching and learning leads are mindful of subject-distortion and appropriate time has been allocated to curriculum development. The coalescence of these conditions is not the norm.

So what, therefore, are the solutions? To my mind, they are threefold:

1. An effort must be made to co-ordinate across policymakers, academics and, crucially, *those working in schools*, to build consensus around terminology. The current discourse around curriculum ultimately feels far away from the struggling early career teacher teaching 22 lessons a week. And yet these are the very people who we *need* to be engaged in conversations

and discussion around school curricula. For that to take place, the above co-ordination on language and concepts must take place, and schools must be given appropriate time to wrestle with these. If the term 'knowledge rich' exists in Ofsted reports, then it must be clearly defined by those who lead on education policy.

2. There is an argument that the term 'knowledge rich' is, in itself, a distraction and that instead the focus should be on grappling with what knowledge looks like within specific subjects. I don't agree that we should cast out the term, but I *do* think that the future of the knowledge movement lies in rich subject communities. The history community is an interesting case study. In the wake of government and Ofsted reforms, many leaders in the community rightly pointed out that knowledge had always had a place in history teaching discourse and curricula (see, for instance, the *Medieval Minds* textbook[19]). But more than this, the history community had already been grappling with the idea of disciplinary knowledge before it appeared in policy discussion. Any history teacher training in the 2000s would have known that enquiry-planning involved a careful blend of substantive knowledge and a clear focus on a particular second-order concept (disciplinary knowledge). The key here is that a rich subject community has allowed for dynamic discussions around knowledge in the curriculum to flourish. For the knowledge turn to be truly successful, we need subject communities across the country and within schools to grow and develop.

3. Initial teacher training (ITT) should play an important role. Recent changes to ITT threaten the subject-specific component of traditional PGCE programmes. This aspect needs to flourish, or the subject communities

we are trying to create will not develop. Were we to take the example of history again, the Ofsted research review for history – a vital document in supporting schools to implement knowledge-rich history curricula – drew heavily on the periodical *Teaching History*.[20] It is not a coincidence that much of the material in *Teaching History* has come from those involved in subject-specific ITT. We need this type of discourse to flourish and thrive.

So in summary, the 2 per cent of truth is that some things clearly have not gone well when it comes to the knowledge-rich curriculum in England. There is work to do around supporting schools in both understanding and implementing curricula that align with knowledge-rich principles. This will take time and should be underpinned by rich subject communities that are free to wrestle with the idea of knowledge in their own subject. This can be accelerated by building world-class subject-specific ITT that develops teachers who think critically about the substance of their teaching.

The limitations of knowledge: A constructive challenger perspective

Jim Knight

It is vital for the success of schooling that the curriculum is thoughtfully designed and sequenced. It is the 'what' of teaching. It is equally important that the curriculum is assessed, both formatively and summatively, so that teachers can be confident that the progression through the sequencing is secure. So, what of the place of knowledge in the curriculum?

Knowledge is fundamental to education. By and large, I agree that knowledge precedes skill. I have no argument with the importance of knowledge acquisition to the cognitive development we want for all children. So, what is the problem with the knowledge-rich curriculum?

When I read around this question, I often find myself in agreement with the advocates of the knowledge-rich curriculum in its theoretical context. My disagreement is with how it has worked in England.

The problem of outcomes in England

Some say that English schools are some of the best in the world. Our place in the PISA (Programme for International Student Assessment) tables went up for reading and maths last time around, and similarly in other international comparative studies.[1,2] I am told that this vindicates the knowledge-rich approach.

This is not the whole story. England's absolute performance in PISA in reading and maths rose between 10 and 11 points, respectively, between 2009 and 2018, but 4 years later fell back to almost where we started in 2009.[3,4,5] In science we have declined.[6] PISA also found that 15-year-olds' 'life satisfaction' had collapsed between 2015 and 2022.[7,8] Across the OECD, England is now second bottom by this measure.[9] This mirrors the attendance crisis blighting our schools, where our 11.8 per cent level of long-term absence is significantly higher than the OECD average of 7.6 per cent.[10,11] This is often blamed on the COVID-19 pandemic. That is all very well, but why are our children impacted more than in other countries that also experienced the global pandemic? There is something about the curriculum, accountability and teaching that is failing to engage too many young people.

We are also failing to engage teachers: 10 per cent of newly qualified teachers leave after their first year.[12] Overall, 40,800 left teaching in English state schools in 2023/24.[13] This is due to a range of factors, but one of them is the curriculum and the associated rigid pedagogy that we now expect from teachers.

Finally, there is very little evidence that the current knowledge-rich approach is delivering the outcomes we need for young people.

The numbers Not in Education, Employment or Training (NEET) rose from 12.1 per cent in 2023 to 13.4 per cent in 2024.[14] At the other end of the achievement scale, the application rate to universities is falling.[15] Productivity in the economy has stalled, frustrating the growth the economy needs that in turn would yield the tax returns required to fund schools properly.

This failure to engage young people is catastrophic for them and for the country. Overall, 35 per cent fail to get at least a grade 4 (a 'standard pass') in English and maths at age 16,[16] that falls to 26 per cent by 18 years old.[17] That quarter of young people then face a bleak future in work and potentially become a drain on the public purse.

Whilst the knowledge-rich curriculum is good in theory in England, in practice it is neither delivering the outcomes to give individuals the opportunities they need, nor delivering the workforce the country needs for a prosperous future. It could be argued that we just need to double down on better teaching of the knowledge-rich curriculum, but with our enduring failure to recruit and retain teachers, I see no prospect of this working. It is time for change.

A better balance

This analysis is familiar. It is well explored in studies by *The Times* Education Commission,[18] HMC,[19] the Tony Blair Institute for Global Change,[20] Cambridge University Press and Assessment[21] and the House of Lords Education for 11–16 Year Olds Committee.[22] All these studies came to similar conclusions.

'Knowledge rich' has been translated into a curriculum that is overwhelmed with content. It is obese. History and geography teachers tell me that they simply do not have the time to cover the whole programme of study at GCSE. Charles Tracy from the Institute of Physics told the Lords Committee:

> The current curriculum in the sciences and in physics is definitely content-rich, and not just content-rich but built on content. Most people think it is probably overloaded with content, sometimes called substantive knowledge. It can leave the impression that physics is a large compendium of disparate facts … we have been working … to develop guidance for a curriculum that explicitly outlines that disciplinary knowledge and those practices and ways of

thinking in the sciences, and does so in a way that builds towards a smaller number of big ideas rather than a large number of small facts.[23]

This obesity may be the fault of the exam boards and their regulators in overloading programmes of study, but the GCSE is a public examination of the national curriculum, which needs a lot of stifling detail to be stripped out. Accompanying changes to the accountability system are also needed to address the criticism of over-testing and too much 'teaching to the test'. As the report from the Tony Blair Institute says:

> High-stakes exams at the end of courses now dominate assessment, which promotes teaching to the test and narrow pedagogies. More than half of schools are starting GCSEs early, further squeezing what pupils learn.[24]

The purpose of schooling

Schooling needs to prepare individuals for personal, social and professional success. Developing knowledge and skills is critical but cannot be the be all and end all. Schooling must also prepare people for worthwhile employment, including vocational skills. It must nurture the creativity, empathy and character needed for people to grow as citizens and in successful relationships. And it must nurture the values and cultural norms for people to thrive on a sustainable planet, in our country and in communities.

Much of this can be acquired through knowledge acquisition. The humanities teach us about our story as a planet and a nation, about how we work socially and how we interact with the natural environment. Neglected parts of the national curriculum like PSHE (personal, social, health and economic) education, citizenship and the arts can then help build other understanding. A change to accountability could quickly re-balance away from the sole focus on the abstract academic knowledge of the EBacc (English Baccalaureate).

When Nick Gibb was schools minister, he appeared before the House of Lords Education for 11–16 Year Olds Committee in 2023. He was asked about the basis of the decision for what to include in the EBacc. He said that 'those are the subjects that are most likely to secure you a place at a high-tariff university'.[25] He went on to explain that this was a social justice issue to incentivise the system to open up access to such universities for more disadvantaged pupils.[26]

This is fair enough in isolation, but in practice, the combination of the EBacc and the knowledge-rich curriculum has crowded out applied learning and the arts. The numbers studying arts subjects to GCSE fell from 13.4 per cent of entries in 2010 to 7.1 per cent in 2024.[27]

The arts and sport both teach the importance of practice, of struggle and of perseverance. They teach teamwork and communication, problem solving and creativity. They are core subjects in delivering the employability skills demanded by the labour market.

This scenario is as striking for vocational and technical qualifications. Young people are faced with a choice at age 16 of continuing with academic learning or opting for technical and vocational qualifications, like T Levels and apprenticeships. Many have no experience of any style of learning other than the academic and therefore inevitably carry on with A levels when they would be more fulfilled and engaged with the other options. Whilst the Wolf review of vocational education[28] stripped out some meaningless qualifications and equivalences, the overall effect has been a reduction of almost a third in vocational learning in the past 10 years.[29]

If we want to address the problems of NEETs, of disengagement, and of productivity, we need to set up apprenticeships and T Levels for success. This requires room to be found in the timetable for vocational, technical and applied learning alongside a core of knowledge.

Schooling for an uncertain future

This analysis has assumed that these decisions about curriculum, assessment and pedagogy take place in a static environment. Yet we have never lived in a more dynamic time of change. It is important to consider whether the knowledge-rich approach in England equips young people to face that future.

Trends would suggest that many of the children in school today will live to 100. Basic economics tells us that generating a big enough pension pot will mean that they will need to continue to earn into their late 70s and early 80s. The idea that the knowledge and skills they learn up to their early 20s will be all they need to thrive for 60 years in a rapidly changing labour market is fanciful.

We need to urgently redesign the whole education system to end the three-stage model of education, then work, then retirement. Learning and earning need to interweave. Universities need to move to business models that incentivise us to return to higher education regularly in adulthood. Colleges need to be closer to employers' and learners' individual development needs. And schools will need to have developed in pupils both a love of learning, but also confidence and resilience so that when their job is replaced by a machine, they have hope that they can take advantage of the new employment opportunities created by technology.

This requires school pedagogy and a curriculum that is grounded in knowledge and skills but that has time for passion-based learning. The EPQ (the Level 3 Extended Project Qualification) is a popular post-16 qualification that allows in-depth work into areas of knowledge. It is also a better predictor of future undergraduate success than the A level. If we want learners to be more empowered explorers of learning, and more self-directed, then we should look to the HPQ (the Level 2 Higher Project Qualification) and the EPQ as a more standard part of key stages 4 and 5.

Some of this change depends on changes to university admissions. For as long as universities admit on the basis of A levels, we will retain the bias towards knowledge-rich academic learning in schools. The opportunity for universities is to adopt digital credentials that can be interrogated more thoroughly. A paper certificate tells us no more than a grade: it doesn't say anything about which parts of the curriculum were secure and which were not. Digital credentials can fix that problem. The digital badging movement[30] has already shown the credibility of having a digital certificate that employers, peers and others can click through to see the evidence behind an award. A widespread adoption of digital portfolios would allow learners to sign over access to their digital certificates to admissions offices and employers, to give a richer sense of an individual's potential and achievement.

A widespread move to digital portfolios then allows for a wider range of qualifications to be studied to reflect a more dynamic world. It can then include other learning and achievements that are harder to assess in objective summative assessment. That is necessary for a more inclusive schools system that values more than knowledge-rich academic learning.

Agile learners

The focus on the knowledge-rich curriculum has been important. We must retain the expertise in teaching reading and maths. We must also continue to focus on curriculum design to deliberately 'scaffold' knowledge, understanding and skills.

However, it is time to move on to a more balanced curriculum that has been slimmed down to give ideas room to breathe, and to enable schools to serve all children. Teachers know their children and their context, and they must be able to design lessons with more variety to keep both themselves and their learners better engaged. This offers the chance to instil curiosity and a passion for learning in all children, and ways to reflect their wider range of achievement.

This shift to a more balanced curriculum is urgent if we are to equip everyone to be agile learners in a dynamic future.

Knowledge and skills: A journey not a dichotomy

Clare Sealy

The ultimate aim of education is to enable children to become better able to think critically, to be creative, to collaborate with others and to solve problems. This aim, this destination, is embraced as much by advocates of a knowledge-rich education as it is by those who argue for the pre-eminence of teaching skills.

This may come as a surprise to advocates of a skills-rich curriculum, who tend to put forward one of two lines of argument. The first sees knowledge and skills in opposition to each other. Here, knowledge is at the very least a distraction from acquiring skills, and possibly antithetical to it. Understandably, given this premise, a knowledge-rich education is seen as profoundly problematic. The second proposition is that skills and knowledge are ingredients that need balancing so that there is neither too much nor too little of one or the other. Knowledge-rich advocacy is therefore seen as unhelpful because the balance is believed to be out of kilter and to the detriment of skill acquisition.

Employers point to the inability of some of their younger, more recent hires to think critically or creatively, or to communicate well or collaborate with others, and reason that this must be because the education they received did not focus enough on teaching such things.[1] The solution they therefore propose seems obvious: transform education by putting skills front and centre.

The case for skills is further strengthened by considering the ubiquity of digital technology with its vast stores of instantly available knowledge and massive processing power. Surely this renders relying on the fragile wetware of the human brain as the go-to repository of information ludicrously outdated?

Some advocates of skills-rich education believe there is a more sinister aspect to knowledge-rich education. They are concerned about knowledge as a means of social control, with the 'knowledge of the powerful' being imparted in order to keep the 'lower orders' from questioning or rebelling against the status quo.

These are real issues that need to be taken seriously. Some young people do seem to lack the ability to communicate and collaborate or to think critically. While education standards in England have risen steadily in the past 15 years and England now compares very favourably in international comparative tests, such as PISA (Programme for International Student Assessment) and TIMSS (Trends in International Mathematics and Science Study), this is because the children whose attainment falls into the middle and higher attainment ranges are doing better.[2,3] There is less improvement for those whose attainment lies in the lower ranges. Such children, disproportionately male,[4] are more likely to grow up into adults feeling disempowered and angry, easier prey to political or ideological extremism. Digital technology does mean that educators need to think hard about how best to harness its power (alongside reducing its potential harms). The rise and rise of the post-truth, conspiracy theory-laden era surely calls for education to equip our children with the ability to think critically about what they are being told on social media.

These are far from trivial issues. It is therefore of the utmost importance that any advocacy of a model for education is based on the very best evidence available. We cannot champion critical thinking and fail to think critically ourselves. We cannot settle on apparently obvious conclusions unless they are warranted by the very best evidence available about how to achieve the aims described above. Yet the advocacy of what could be called a skills-rich approach is not based on secure evidence and rests on a confusion of ends with means. Belief in critical thinking as an endpoint becomes conflated with reducing the curriculum to its ultimate goals rather than describing how to actually get there. Put simply, one does not learn how to think critically, or problem solve or be creative by being taught a curriculum that directly focuses on these things. While one can see how this might appear to be logical at first glance, when we dig deeper beyond what feels like it must be true, we find there is indisputable evidence, both scientific and in practice, that refutes this.

The overwhelming consensus within the field of cognitive science in recent decades is that knowledge plays a crucial role in thinking. Psychologist Daniel Willingham explains this well:

> Data from the last thirty years lead to a conclusion that is not scientifically challengeable: thinking well requires knowing facts, and that's true not simply because you need something to think about. The very processes that teachers care about most – critical thinking processes such as reasoning and problem solving – are intimately intertwined with factual knowledge that is stored in long-term memory (not just found in the environment).[5]

As educational psychologists Paul A. Kirschner, John Sweller and Richard E. Clark explain in their 2006 article:

Our understanding of the role of long-term memory in human cognition has altered dramatically over the last few decades. It is no longer seen as a passive repository of discrete, isolated fragments of information that permit us to repeat what we have learned. Nor is it seen only as a component of human cognitive architecture that has merely peripheral influence on complex cognitive processes such as thinking and problem solving. Rather, long-term memory is now viewed as the central, dominant structure of human cognition. Everything we see, hear, and think about is critically dependent on and influenced by our long-term memory.[6]

If we want our children to be able to think critically and solve problems, we therefore need them to acquire the knowledge that will enable them to do so. This is categorically not an argument for rote learning long lists of disconnected facts that a child is expected to regurgitate in exams. On the contrary, it is about building interconnected webs of knowledge that allow for meaning making. This is why the most recent Ofsted school inspection handbook[7] expected schools to have a coherent curriculum in place that develops concepts over time, gradually introducing children to examples of increasing complexity, nuance and depth. A knowledge-rich curriculum is the antithesis of an exam-rich curriculum where children are taught exam rubrics and mark schemes rather than rich and meaningful knowledge.

The argument that digital technology now allows us to circumvent knowing stuff ourselves, because we can outsource that to a digital other, is similarly not grounded in evidence. Making sense of the torrent of digital information in our lives requires a knowledge base in order to sort the wheat from the chaff. Without knowledge, one is highly likely to become confused, jump to erroneous conclusions and, if you learn anything, run the risk of learning things that are at best incorrect or incomplete and at worst deeply biased. E. D. Hirsch explains this in his article entitled '"You can always look it up" … or can you?':

> There is a consensus in cognitive psychology that it takes knowledge to gain knowledge. Those who repudiate a fact-filled curriculum on the grounds that kids can always look things up miss the paradox that de-emphasizing factual knowledge actually disables children from looking things up effectively. To stress process at the expense of factual knowledge actually hinders children from learning to learn. Yes, the Internet has placed a wealth of information at our fingertips. But to be able to use that information – to absorb it, to add to our knowledge – we must already possess a storehouse of knowledge. That is the paradox disclosed by cognitive research.[8]

Over-reliance on the internet instead of thinking things through oneself has other downsides. It decreases the kind of productive cognitive effort that engenders learning, and can suppress creative potential.[9] AI might be able to produce results much faster than we can, but it is the *process* of writing, or solving a maths problem or drawing that develops the ability to think like an author or a mathematician or an artist.

What is more, for the past 15 or so years, the UK has unwittingly been carrying out its own quasi-experiment into the relative superiority of a knowledge-rich versus skills-rich approach to education. England has followed the knowledge-rich path and risen up the international league tables, whereas Scotland and Wales have adopted skills-rich approaches and seen their results plunge. Scotland's unfortunately named 'Curriculum for Excellence' was deliberately organised around content-free skills, an approach that Keir Bloomer, one of its architects, now regrets: 'The problem is we did not make sufficiently clear that skills are the accumulation of knowledge. Without knowledge there can be no skills.'[10]

Given that both the scientific consensus and lessons from history clearly demonstrate that a skills-led, knowledge-light curriculum is highly unlikely to be successful in achieving the aims its advocates cherish, it is common for the argument to switch to discussion of what is the most appropriate balance between knowledge and skills. This rests on a misconception about what skills are. What research tells us is that skills are the result of orchestrating many smaller parts together. The reason that trying to teach a complex skill doesn't work for most learners is that human cognitive architecture is such that it can't cope with lots of new information at once. The place where we think – often called working memory – is limited in capacity and easily overwhelmed. Effective teaching therefore relies on breaking down a complex skill into its constituent parts and then, over time, gradually combining these together into more complex activities. These constituent parts are what we mean by knowledge.

A common metaphor for this journey from knowledge to skills is that of the journey from ingredients to cake. A cake is relatively complex, being made out of smaller parts – ingredients. When making a cake, you don't need a balance of ingredients and cake, you need to start with ingredients and gradually combine them together until you end up with a cake.

This explains why a knowledge-light curriculum is particularly harmful for children with cognition and learning special educational needs who are likely to have a smaller working memory than their peers. In its guidance *Special educational needs in mainstream schools,*[11] the Education

Endowment Foundation surveyed contemporary research on the most effective approaches to teaching children with special educational needs and found that explicit teaching – teaching where knowledge is broken down into small steps and taught directly – is fundamental to children with cognition and learning difficulties learning successfully. It is children with the lowest prior attainment in Scotland who have been disproportionately harmed by the impact of the 'Curriculum for Excellence'. Where a curriculum removes content in the mistaken belief that this is a sure route to skills, it is the children with the lowest starting points who suffer the most. Conversely, a knowledge-rich curriculum, taught well, provides the most inclusive kind of curriculum.

'Taught well' is important. Advocates of skills-rich education may well fear that knowledge-rich education means a 'transmission' model where the teacher imparts information in lecture style with little interaction from pupils and little checking whether or not they have understood what has been taught or changing tack if they have not. This is not what a knowledge-rich education should involve. It should be highly interactive, with frequent checking for understanding with the teacher responding in the moment where it is apparent that children do not yet understand.

Like Scotland, though to a far less extensive degree, England still has too many children in the lowest bands of educational achievement.[12,13] It cannot be the curriculum that is the problem here though, given that this problem is experienced in both Scotland and England despite the big differences in educational approach. The cause is more likely to lie in something they hold in common. One possible candidate could be the years of austerity that have undermined welfare systems in the UK. It could be argued that the fact that, on average, children in England have performed better internationally despite the demise of a robust safety-net is down to the protective effects of a knowledge-rich curriculum, which their Scottish counterparts have sadly not enjoyed.

A knowledge-rich curriculum is one in which schools are custodians, curators and critics of the intellectual and cultural legacy of humankind. The storehouse of human knowledge is immense. Some of that content is so powerful and so important that it must be preserved and nurtured at all costs for future generations – for example, technologies of writing and calculation. Some of the storehouse's content requires schools to make judicious choices about teaching this rather than that – since one can only ever teach the tiniest fragment of all that could potentially be taught. Which books, which periods in history, which case studies in geography, which artists or musicians or materials or techniques? This is where the school as curator works to devise a coherent and meaningful offer that builds on the past while looking to the future. Some of the content in the storehouse of human knowledge requires critiquing the vested interests of the past and giving children the tools to do the same.

Opposition to a knowledge-rich vision of education is often built on a misunderstanding of what it entails. It is not about lecturing children or cramming facts for exams. A knowledge-rich education aims to enable children to think critically and creatively, to solve problems, to communicate effectively and to collaborate with others. It shares this vision for education with those who advocate a skills-led approach. Where it differs, is in providing a more rigorously researched approach as to how these aims are most effectively achieved.

Building a strong knowledge-rich curriculum: What does a well-sequenced knowledge-rich primary curriculum look like?

Emma Lennard

I recently had the opportunity to visit the beautiful cathedral city of Lichfield in Staffordshire. As the train hurtled through the English countryside, I decided to learn more about the place I was visiting. As many of us do daily, much like a reflex, I pulled out my phone and searched 'Lichfield history'. I was offered an AI overview of the history of the city of Lichfield, which I began to scroll through. To paraphrase, it explained that:

- *Lichfield was once the ecclesiastical centre of Mercia.* (I have some basic knowledge of Anglo-Saxon kingdoms from my work with schools developing primary history, so I understood this part to a degree.)
- *The town's ladder-shaped street pattern was laid out in the 12th century.* (I thought this was interesting and made a mental note to look at a map.)
- *In the 18th century, Lichfield was a thriving coaching city home to Samuel Johnson, poet, writer and essayist, and David Garrick, actor, playwright and theatre manager.* (I've been to the Garrick Theatre in London, so there was a connection there for me. I began to imagine a city with a flourishing arts scene.)

- *During the American Revolution, Lichfield served as a supply point and rest stop for American troops travelling to Boston.*

Something didn't seem right with that last point. Were there American troops over here in England during the American Revolution? Why would a city in Staffordshire be used as a supply point? My very basic knowledge of this period of history set off some alarm bells. I then searched further and found Litchfield, Connecticut – named after Lichfield, England – which was, in fact, a supply point during the American Revolution. I had been correct: the AI overview had merged the history of two places with a similar name.

I begin my essay with this anecdote, not to highlight the current limitations of AI but to show an example of critical thinking in action. I could pause, check for sense and then clarify the mistake that was included in the AI overview because I had background knowledge. We can only question things we read, information we become aware of, and stories we hear if we have some knowledge, some truth, that enables us to think critically. If I had not had some background knowledge, basic as it is, I would have accepted that Lichfield had a role in the American Revolution. That mistake, that misconception, would have formed part of my understanding, lying in wait to trip me up in the future.

Those of you reading this with excellent knowledge of history might be thinking 'Oh come on, you are a teacher; surely that mistake was obvious to you!', and you might deride the loss of knowledge in the profession. But we only know what we know; without knowledge, we are left vulnerable to accepting any information as fact. This is what drives my work as an independent curriculum consultant. Our children are growing up in an age where information is more accessible than ever before. Many of them carry devices in their pockets that place them seconds away from all the information that is known, or has ever been known. With a child who is interested in space? A quick search will show you a NASA image of the Orion Nebula, 1,500 light years away, where stars are being born, just while we wait for our bus. Need an interesting animal fact for show and tell while your child eats their morning cereal? Another quick search and we can read about the immortal jellyfish, a fascinating creature that can reverse its life cycle. What a time for us to be alive, with so much to learn.

Perhaps the next logical step, then, is to think we don't need to teach children much any more; they can just 'Google' it. We don't need them to remember endless facts; they can just find them out for themselves. However, with all the information now readily available to children, an important warning comes. Not everything on the internet is true. Along with simple mistakes, erroneous information can have a darker side. It is now more important than ever that children are taught about the world around them; its past, the way it works now, how everything within it is connected. We need knowledgeable, confident children who have had space within their education to reflect and form opinions. This will help them see mistakes, develop a perception for misinformation and envisage a future they can actively shape. As those invested in education, it is our obligation to make this a reality for all children, no matter their background.

The responsibility to fulfil this obligation to our children is huge, but we can do much of this work in schools, with children at the start of their education. We can design a primary curriculum that contains the very best ingredients: rich knowledge, opportunities to develop vital skills and experiences that provide insight into the world around us. In creating a curriculum that seeks out truth, we arm children with weapons to fight against misinformation and support the development of their ability to think critically.

But what does this actually look like? How do children learn to think critically in primary school? In my work with schools nationwide, I have seen huge variety in both curriculum clarity and content. In some cases, the content of the primary school curriculum is largely left up to individual teachers and there is little communication about what to include and in what order. Often in these cases there have been other priorities, and the curriculum has taken a back seat. In science, children might grow cress seeds 3 years in a row when they study plants, because cress seeds are inexpensive and quick to grow. However, with some thought to the sequencing of content, when learning about plants, children could grow cress seeds, then the following year they could watch mung beans germinate, then the following year they could grow sunflowers. This sequencing, putting curriculum content into a logical order, supports children to learn more, widening and deepening their understanding – for example of plants – over time.

The workload of researching, planning and delivering over 10 subjects, as we do in primary schools, can easily become an impossible task. Where schools have curriculum clarity, teachers and school leaders know what is taught, when and why. This enables them to ensure that the sequence of the curriculum supports children to make progress over time.

You may be thinking: but we have a national curriculum, isn't that enough? The national curriculum provides high-level statements that do, in many respects, provide focus for schools. However, there is a still a huge amount of work to be done to translate national curriculum statements into what actually happens in a classroom. As an example:

> • *locate the world's countries, using maps to focus on Europe (including the location of Russia) and North and South America, concentrating on their environmental regions, key physical and human characteristics, countries, and major cities*
>
> (National curriculum framework document, 2013)[1]

A teacher might reflect on this in the following ways:

- 'We have to study countries in Europe, but which ones? All of them? Do children know about any countries in Europe already?'
- 'How much detail should children know about the countries of Europe? Are we teaching them about the location, the landscape, industry, trade? Do children understand what trade is?'
- 'What are the main environmental regions of North and South America? What should children know about each of these?'
- 'Which human characteristics of Europe should we choose to study? Can children read population maps? Do children need to know about politics? Shall we pick some famous landmarks to study?'
- 'Shall we study Washington DC or Mexico City? Do we have time to study both? Have children learned about population before?'
- 'Which of North America's rivers is most important to learn about, or should we study mountain ranges?'
- 'I want to teach the children about the Andes Mountains, the Atacama Desert and the Amazon River in South America; have they learned about mountains, deserts and rivers before?'

One of the key lines of questioning above refers to prior knowledge; what do children already know about the thing we want them to learn? Psychologist David Ausubel asserts that 'The most important single factor influencing learning is what the learner already knows. Ascertain this and teach [them] accordingly.'[2]

If children are going to learn about the Mississippi River in North America, it is helpful to know what children already know about rivers. They may know about a local river. They may know the different parts of a river as it journeys from its source to its mouth. Perhaps the children have studied the water cycle and understand how water moves within it. Do children already understand how humans interact with rivers – for example, what irrigation is?

As you can see, an individual teacher working alone would have a substantial task ahead of them if they wanted to turn national curriculum statements, such as the one outlined above, into lesson plans for every subject they teach.

Alongside the challenging task of deciding exactly what we want children to learn, we also need to consider the order in which we teach it. When we think about the learning sequence, we establish a deliberate order. This supports learning by creating strong, purposeful foundations. A sequenced curriculum will support children to build on their knowledge and remember what they have learned.

Take the following example: in order for children in year 5 to successfully use a relief map (a map that shows the height of land), they must first understand what a simple map is. To help children understand simple maps, it is useful for them to first look at aerial views. This will support their early conceptual understanding of what a map represents, before moving on to interacting with more complex maps. A sequence is emerging here, whereby we think carefully about what children need to know in order to gain competence and confidence in the knowledge and skills we are focused on. If a year 5 teacher attempts to teach relief maps and realises children are unfamiliar with some of the basic skills needed to map read, such as identifying compass directions, they will have to adjust their lesson plan and teach the prerequisite skills. Otherwise, children are unlikely to succeed. In the same way, map projection, taught in years 5 and 6, relies on a good understanding of world maps and globes. Without this, the concept of taking a 3D globe and creating a flat map will be difficult to understand.

Figure 1: A sequenced curriculum: Map work

Early years foundation stage (EYFS):	Years 1 and 2:	Years 3 and 4:	Years 5 and 6:
My community, my local area, travel around the world, explorers, North Pole and South Pole (globes)	My classroom, my school site, drawing maps, my local area, aerial views, compass points, drawing maps with features of the local area, planning a route, globes	Maps, compasses, symbols, grid references, fieldwork, contrasting localities, globes, tropics, map scales	Hemispheres, scale, co-ordinates, relief maps, latitude, longitude, time zones, map projection, world maps

A well-sequenced curriculum benefits all children, but especially children for whom learning presents particular challenges. What we know has a direct impact on what we learn. Melbourne University's John Hattie and South Australia University's Gregory Yates have found through their research that 'Prior knowledge has a bigger impact on learning than differences in IQ.'[3]

It is clear that existing knowledge is important, acting as a foundation for future learning. Teachers need to establish what children already understand and then target their teaching to build on this foundation. If a teacher notices that children's existing knowledge is not secure, they must adapt their teaching to secure the knowledge that children need before they move on. Teachers can only do this if they are working within a well-sequenced curriculum, where content has been clearly specified and put into an order that supports learning over time.

For another example, let's look at primary history. It could be the case that a school decides that children will study the Romans in year 4. A teacher could plan a 6-week unit of history focused on the Romans where children learn about the Roman Empire, get to go on a trip to a local significant site, learn about some features of Roman towns (such as baths) and study the story of Boudica's uprising against the Romans.

> • *the Roman Empire and its impact on Britain*
>
>   (National curriculum framework document, 2013)[4]

Children are very likely to enjoy learning about the Romans, and the content of the curriculum will be brought to life with the trip to a local significant site. But while this may be an interesting episode of learning here, is it part of a series? What happens if the children never return to this knowledge? It is likely to be forgotten. Within a well-sequenced curriculum, children will revisit content they've previously learned, and they will later encounter content that builds on this knowledge. An example is outlined on the next page.

Useful prior knowledge	Current knowledge	Possible future knowledge
• Location of Italy • Location of Europe • Location of the Alps • Location of the countries of the UK, including the border between England and Scotland • Features of modern towns • Anglo-Saxon England	• The spread of the Roman Empire • Features of Roman towns • Hadrian's Wall • Boudica's uprising	• Other empires such as the Mongol Empire • The spread of Christianity within the Roman Empire • Other ancient civilisations such as ancient Greece • Understanding how power is gained and lost

Within a well-sequenced curriculum, children could encounter important concepts such as power, justice and culture in many different historical contexts, deepening their understanding. These encounters must be well planned for and not left to chance. If children understand how empires have developed and fallen in the past, they will make connections to events happening in the world today.

In their book on insights from psychology for teaching, David Didau and Nick Rose write: 'The more you know, the more complex and interesting the connection you can make.'[5] Knowledge is important for children to make connections, but it is also important for them to be able to spot, as I did with Lichfield, where a connection doesn't seem to make sense. We know how to choose curriculum content carefully and sequence it meaningfully. If we ensure that this is implemented, our children will enter into the next phase of their education, and into the world, armed with knowledge to think critically, navigate challenges and effect change.

Phonics and a knowledge-rich approach: Developing a phonics programme that delivers vocabulary and language knowledge alongside code knowledge

Tara Dodson

Every child deserves to learn to read and to love reading, regardless of their background. This was our motivation when Katie Press and I were developing our systematic synthetic phonics (SSP) programme, Essential Letters and Sounds (ELS).[1]

Phonics involves teaching that the sounds we make within our language link to a written piece of code – letters – on a page. We learn each of these pieces of code to be able to read. When we read, we decode; and when we spell, we encode. In phonics, we are therefore always teaching 'knowledge', as we teach children the pieces of code that make up our language and how to apply this knowledge when reading.

We know that effective teaching of early reading skills – that is, teaching how to decode and blend sounds when reading, alongside teaching language and vocabulary to ensure comprehension – allows children to better understand the diverse curricula on offer within schools. Reading is therefore a key indicator of future success. For example, children who achieve their early learning goal[2] for literacy are significantly more likely to achieve the expected outcomes in *numeracy* at the end of key stage 2.

Research undertaken in both the UK and internationally shows that teaching phonics as part of a language-rich curriculum is recognised to be the most effective instruction for the teaching of early reading.[3] The 2006 independent Rose Review of early reading teaching, for example, found high-quality phonics teaching to be the fastest route for the vast majority of children to become a skilled reader.[4] The review showed that diluting the teaching of phonics almost always inhibited the outcomes of the learner.

In 2021, the Department for Education's new reading framework was released, alongside an updated list of SSP programmes validated for funding as part of the English Hubs Programme.[5] The English Hubs Programme is a Department for Education initiative to provide funding, training and support to improve the teaching of early literacy with a particular focus on SSP, reading for pleasure and early language development. ELS is one of the validated programmes. The support available to schools through the literacy specialists based at each English Hub ensures that teachers are equipped to deliver their chosen SSP to achieve the best outcomes.

According to Ofsted's national director for education, Lee Owston, 'Extensive research shows how important teaching systematic synthetic phonics (SSP) is until children can decode automatically.'[6] Further support is therefore now being developed to help secondary schools to close existing gaps in knowledge for children for whom early reading was not taught in a robust and successful way. When developing our ELS programme, we drew upon research that shows how learners learn best. For example, by simplifying the procedures within lessons, we saw that children were more engaged and knew how to respond within each part of the lesson. Cognitive load theory[7] explains how we process and use information, and we found this supported our findings within our trial schools. We all have limited capacity for working memory, which means that we want to use as little extraneous information as possible when teaching, to allow children to focus on the core content of the lesson. Teachers should avoid overwhelming a child's working memory, as this can distract from the core content. Instead, we should focus on creating meaningful connections with a child's existing knowledge and integrating new knowledge, to allow them to apply their understanding in a deeper way, leading to better long-term retention of the knowledge.

For our ELS programme we therefore developed four very simple lesson plans. These are rigid and used to teach specific types of lessons or parts of the progression where there is a requirement for a different activity. The expectation on the children and the teacher is clear and consistent. Children can focus on the content of the lesson without being distracted by changes to the structure of the lesson. In contrast, some phonics programmes have a flexible lesson structure and use differing activities within lessons, meaning that children may need to adapt to a change in the lesson's structure as well as remember how to complete each of the activities that may be used. In our ELS programme, the clarity of the lesson's objectives – to learn a new grapheme-phoneme correspondence (GPC) (the correspondence between spellings and sounds in English) *or* to practise using GPCs that the children already know – are always the same. Children therefore attend each lesson secure in their understanding of what will happen. This is one way in which our ELS programme reduces cognitive load and allows children to learn better. Consistent terminology is also used by all staff who teach early reading using ELS, and this is written on the whiteboard for every lesson – the correct terminology will therefore always be used, even if a supply teacher is delivering the lesson. Children learn the routines of the lesson, and this secure model means that they know what to expect within their first few weeks of primary school.

English is a challenging language to learn, as there are around 44 sounds but many ways to spell these sounds. This means that learners of English must fluently recognise the 175 common spellings for these sounds but also be aware of the less common spellings. English contains multiple sounds for letters and multiple spellings for sounds. We have more than 200 ways to spell the sounds within our language and some of these spellings are only ever used once. Other languages have simpler sound-to-spelling structures, meaning that there is less to learn, thereby making the language more accessible.

The complexity of the code of our language therefore means that children need continued and sustained practice beyond the initial teaching. The first time a sound (phoneme) and corresponding spelling (grapheme) are introduced, children should be supported to apply this new knowledge. Subsequent practice of this knowledge then allows children to independently recognise the new grapheme and use it when they are decoding independently. This is a skill that takes repeated practice. It can be achieved with short bursts of teaching and reviewing outside of the lesson; reading words that are familiar; reading new words; reading sentences and books that contain newly taught graphemes; and reading pseudo words to support consistent recognition of GPCs.

This continuous rehearsal of existing knowledge (previously taught content) allows children to master their application of this knowledge. This is a key identifying feature of a 'knowledge-rich' curriculum, but is also simply good practice. Spaced retrieval practice allows children to build on prior knowledge by revisiting and applying it within a new context. As the Education Endowment Foundation's Alex Quigley notes, a curriculum:

> … must be well-sequenced and underpinned by an understanding of how children learn … in addition, it must be based on a rich conception of knowledge that includes the skills and attitudes that contribute to success.[8]

Where children require additional practice outside of the main teaching, we developed an in-lesson intervention in our phonics programme to make the most of teaching time to close any gaps. The in-lesson intervention within ELS focuses on sound manipulation and listening for the GPC within the word, then identifying its correct placement before building the word. This is an adult-led activity to support children who find learning to apply their new knowledge more challenging. There are three further interventions that teach specific knowledge and then give children additional opportunity to apply their knowledge. By developing children's reading skills alongside their ability to decode (recognise the GPCs within each word), we develop children who are engaged in reading and therefore read more and learn more.

When developing ELS, we looked to other knowledge bases and studies that proved that knowledge accompanied by context equals better outcomes. As noted, in phonics we are always teaching 'knowledge' as we teach children to determine the pieces of code that make up our language and how to apply these in each word. Children's understanding of GPCs is built slowly with explicit focus on learning them, and then on independently applying their understanding of them. Over time this supports children to build an orthographic map[9] – a concrete model of the way sounds are spelled within words and which sounds can be represented by specific spellings. Exposure to lots of text and providing opportunities to practise applying knowledge of GPCs is key.

Teaching GPC knowledge in isolation, without context and vocabulary knowledge, is not enough. This does not create 'good' or fluent readers. Philip Gough and William Tunmer's 'simple view of reading'[10] shows us that children's ability to decode and their active language knowledge can determine their rate of comprehension. When developing ELS, we therefore knew that we needed to also specifically give children vocabulary knowledge so that when they are applying their GPC understanding, they can also comprehend the texts they encounter. This helps us to provide a more equitable base for all children to begin their reading journey. For children who have perhaps not had the same input before arriving at school, it is key that their phonics lessons include the meaning of vocabulary needed to engage with the school curriculum. We wanted to include this vocabulary, and knowledge of its use, to allow schools to support children to become *readers* rather than *decoders*. This goes beyond the standard model for an SSP: not all programmes provide context or understanding for the words, captions, phrases or sentences that are read within a lesson. Every ELS lesson provides children with not only the GPC knowledge or practice of GPC knowledge, but also the chance to re-read familiar words. This enables children to read words effortlessly, alongside applying their understanding of the meaning of words.

We opted to include teaching word knowledge in our ELS programme by providing illustrations for every word (that was possible to illustrate) read within the lesson. Studies show that children who have the corresponding image for the word pointed to while being read to gain more vocabulary knowledge.[11] The images – which are very specific to each word – provide immediate context and ensure that all children have had the same access to the language and vocabulary through explicit instruction. Where a word is too complex to illustrate, teachers are asked to use the word in context. For example, you cannot illustrate the word 'much': therefore, the teacher might give varied examples such as 'How much does this cost?', 'How much did it weigh?' and 'There's so much ice cream!'. The teacher can then explain that 'much' is used to describe an amount or quantity.

Giving children code knowledge alongside developing their language and vocabulary is central to our ELS programme. We want children to lift words off the page *and* take meaning from their reading. Without these two elements of knowledge being given to children, they would be unable to make sense of texts when they come to practise reading.

As a whole-class teaching model, rather than a homogeneous groupings model, ELS ensures that all children access the same vocabulary and language. This means that children from lower socio-economic status groups, who are most at risk of starting school with lower levels of language and communication, are exposed to the same language as their peers and are supported by the teacher to understand its use. As Ofsted has stated, 'Language is the bedrock of thinking and learning',[12] and language and communication skills are the biggest predictors of school achievement.[13,14,15] We therefore developed an SSP that would provide a rigorous introduction to the code of our language alongside an introduction to vocabulary that is used both colloquially and within school curricula.

In any 'knowledge-rich' curriculum, it is vital that the application of that knowledge is practised, and that children are explicitly shown how to use the knowledge that they have been taught. Children will not inherently understand the use of newly taught information unless they are taught how to apply their understanding of the new knowledge and supported until they can do this independently. Hence, when developing the outcomes for each lesson in our programme, we determined that children should first practise with the teacher to use these GPCs within words that are accompanied by illustrations before moving to reading new GPCs within captions, phrases and sentences that also include previously taught GPCs. It was important that these were illustrated, as it allowed us to deliver vocabulary and language knowledge as well as context for meaning. This approach allowed a secure model for this practice, with children then asked to independently apply their understanding having had the activity modelled to them.

Ultimately, as Alex Quigley highlights, 'a successful knowledge-rich curriculum should be designed to help pupils remember what they have been taught'.[16] ELS is built on a success model; children are not asked to do something before they have been *shown how to do it* and have practised it together with their teacher. It is not a test: we teach children how to apply their understanding and knowledge, and to practise this repeatedly until they have mastered it.

Whilst phonics is commonly accepted to be the most effective way to teach children to read and to therefore create readers who enjoy reading, it is essential that the teaching of phonics forms one part of a rich and diverse curriculum that promotes reading and provides opportunities for children to engage with high-quality fiction and non-fiction. Teachers' knowledge of *how* to teach reading should complement their understanding of how to *engage* children in reading.

By providing the framework of code and language knowledge and the ability to apply these skills during their phonics lessons, teachers can then use these skills across the curriculum. Children who read more, learn more and bring more background knowledge to their learning. For me, this is what a 'knowledge-rich' phonics programme provides – a framework that not only teaches children *how* to read, but that also gives them the knowledge to ensure that it all 'makes sense' when they come to read outside of their phonics lessons.

A knowledge-rich approach to art: A primary school case study

Naomi Pilling

The question of how to teach arts subjects with a 'knowledge-rich' approach provokes a degree of anxiety. This stems from the idea that 'knowledge' and 'creativity' are diametrically opposed, or at least somehow in conflict. Having taught art using a knowledge-rich curriculum in primary schools for many years, I would say that such a view is mistaken. It presupposes that how we define 'knowledge' in art is very narrow, relating only to facts rather than the practice of process or skills. However, a good education in art combines all these elements, encouraging children to encounter the rich, varied and exciting creativity of others and use that experience to drive and inform their own creative responses.

What is knowledge in the subject of art? The 2023 Ofsted research review for art and design splits knowledge into three domains: practical knowledge ('about developing technical proficiency'), theoretical knowledge ('the cultural and contextual content that pupils learn about artists and artwork') and disciplinary knowledge ('what pupils learn about how art is studied, discussed and judged').[1] This definition points to the fact that the subject of art is not just about accumulating facts but 'rather … develop[ing] knowledge networks', which allows children to learn by making connections between encountering other peoples' art and what they themselves create.[2] It is no coincidence that this, in fact, is how most professional artists themselves work. They do not create work in a vacuum but learn and are influenced by artwork that they themselves encounter or seek out. Studying the work of other artists fosters their own creativity.

We often encounter the human imagination at its best from the minds of young children at primary school. Indeed, to paraphrase Pablo Picasso, 'Every child is an artist, the problem is how to remain an artist once we grow up.' Harnessing and developing creativity is not just a *nice* thing. It is a part of developing as a rounded human being and, I believe, crucial to our mental wellbeing. Part of being human is to create. It is no wonder that in the isolation of the COVID-19 pandemic people noticeably re-engaged with the arts. Kurt Vonnegut captures the importance of creating when he writes:

> Practice any art, music, singing, dancing, acting, drawing, painting, sculpting, poetry, fiction, essays, reportage, no matter how well or badly, not to get money and fame, but to experience becoming, to find out what's inside you, to make your soul grow.[3]

Practical knowledge

Some approaches to an education in art mistake the desire to promote creativity in the classroom with an absence of explicit teaching. Children may be encouraged to explore a creative response in drawing, painting or sculpture without being given the tools to successfully understand how the materials they are using work. Such an approach can lead to frustration and disappointment on the part of a child and lead them to conclude that art is not for them. Instead, we need to explicitly teach children the skills required in using materials to enable them to succeed and take pleasure in what they have created. Using clay is a case in point. A child may confidently and expressively experiment with manipulating clay, but if they are not explicitly instructed to cross-hatch and apply slip when joining clay together they will experience the disappointment of encountering a broken object once the clay has dried.

'Modelling' (a teacher demonstrating techniques and practices to children) is therefore a key part of teaching art in primary schools to ensure that children acquire the practical knowledge and technical proficiency to be able to express themselves. To reach technical proficiency in using a variety of materials, children need to be shown, in detail, how to use those materials. Any successful curriculum will carefully sequence how those skills are built up, week to week, term to term and year to year. Those teaching art, who in the vast majority of cases are classroom teachers and not art specialists (and commonly lack confidence in teaching the subject), need professional development to ensure that they have secure subject knowledge in order to successfully implement any such curriculum.

Examples of how to learn various drawing and painting techniques illustrate the point. Using lines, whether with pencil, ink, charcoal or any other media, is akin to an artist's basic tool. Children will naturally, and without the need for instruction, find the outside shape of something they observe and may then proceed to colouring in that shape, to try to give it form and detail. They are unlikely, however, to discover spontaneously how lines can be used *within* a shape to create the illusion of form and detail. By observing how the artist Rembrandt (Harmenszoon van Rijn) used cross-hatching and following a teacher who demonstrates how they can use this technique themselves, children can learn a way in which they can create the illusion of three-dimensional form using line. For most children, achieving such an effect requires close attention to instruction and practice. A teacher will need to explicitly demonstrate how to hold the pencil to produce fluid lines, and to use varying pressure and proximity of hatched lines to create areas that vary in tone. Not only are instruction and practice needed to achieve such pencil control, but guiding children to carefully observe shape and the effect of light over shape, before they even put their pencil on the page, is necessary for children to succeed in communicating in their art what they see in front of them.

Similarly, children can begin to understand how lines can be used to show visual texture (how a two-dimensional surface can create the illusion of how a surface feels) by looking at the work of Vincent van Gogh. They can then utilise the technique of using varied marks to replicate texture that they observe in a real object when they draw it. Once again, such techniques require explicit instruction and practice in both observation and execution.

Explicit instruction and practice are also paramount in learning the art of painting. Acrylic paints and watercolour paints, both widely used in primary schools, have entirely different qualities. Acrylics are traditionally treated as an opaque material, whilst watercolours have a translucent quality. Traditionally opaque materials are applied in layers, starting with the darkest and finishing with the lightest (working from 'dark to light') to build up depth of colour. Such an approach allows a pupil to achieve this depth when they seek to show changes of tone in a still life. Conversely, watercolours are traditionally used in the opposite manner, where pigment made translucent by adding water is applied using lightest colours first and then applying layers of darker colours (working from 'light to dark'). Here, a depth of colour showing varying tonal values is achieved in exactly the opposite way from an opaque material. Teaching children established methods such as these allows them to create images in which they can find satisfaction, and from which, of course, they can depart should they want to explore other ways of working.

This is not to say that teaching technique alone constitutes an appropriately varied body of knowledge to support an education in art. Children need to be encouraged and guided in the art of expressing themselves. Creativity at its core is about the expression of self. Any good curriculum will provide a balance of tasks that allows for a development of technique *and* an opportunity to use the imagination with freedom of expression. A child who has acquired an understanding of how different materials work in a variety of ways can explore whether they want to use or depart from those techniques to meet their own expressive ends. For example, a child who has learnt about how different colours, shapes and lines work together in pictorial space, and has practised different techniques of applying paint to the picture plane, can use this knowledge to practise or depart from learnt techniques to effect their unique expressive intentions in an abstract work of art.

Theoretical knowledge

Learning how to use different materials with technical proficiency, and using or departing from these techniques in order to create artwork, is one part of what constitutes knowledge in art. A rich network of knowledge can be developed if this practice is connected with theoretical knowledge.

Theoretical knowledge in this context can mean knowledge of artists, their work, its cultural context, and concepts that relate to their work. Such knowledge is what has been described as 'powerful knowledge', which allows children to go beyond their own experiences.[4] Curriculum design here is crucial. The present early years foundation stage statutory framework and national curriculum at key stages 1 and 2 offer no specificity about which artists and designers teachers should present to children. Instead, it is only stated that teachers should ensure that all pupils 'know about great artists, craft makers and designers, and understand the historical and cultural development of their art forms'.[5] Such a lack of guidance, whilst perhaps allowing flexibility, requires teachers to have secure subject knowledge if children are to be offered a carefully sequenced curriculum that demonstrates breadth and depth, and connects the artistic skills they learn themselves with relevant artistic concepts and developments in artistic style.

What teachers choose to present for study is of course open to debate, and subject to opinion and personal preference. Art should not be the study of a static body of work; as a discipline, it is continually developing and evolving. Recent debates about diversity and decolonisation within the museum and gallery community highlight shifting opinions about what might be considered before a work is included in any 'canon'. This only goes to show the difficulty of pinning down what art we should present to children.

The difficulty of the task, however, does not mean that we should shy away from codifying a curriculum that builds children's knowledge over time. We should strive to provide children with an understanding of the rich and exciting world of visual expression that has existed through history and continues to develop in the 21st century. My experience is that children benefit from an approach to studying art that tries to present a balanced history, reaching back through time from the present, and across geographical and cultural boundaries. In this way, children not only discover a rich world of visual experimentation beyond their own experience, but one that also reflects their own cultural context.

Study of a varied body of work allows children to build a solid schema of understanding about common concepts that relate to that work, allowing them to make connections between different areas of knowledge and build secure understanding. Art is commonly analysed by understanding the principal constituent elements or parts (colour, line, shape, form, tone, space and texture) that make up a whole design. Such elements, which we might think of as the building blocks of art, can be used to analyse what goes into creating 'style' in art. For example, Edvard Munch is commonly understood to have been an expressionist: a movement in which artists sought to express emotions rather than physical reality. By analysing his famous work The Scream of Nature (commonly known as The Scream), children can explore how Edvard Munch's use of swirling lines and complementary colours create a design that conveys an unsettled feeling.

Disciplinary knowledge

By exploring how, for example, Edvard Munch's style is seeking to convey particular emotions, pupils are engaging with what has been referred to as disciplinary knowledge in art, or 'how art is studied, discussed and judged'.[6] One might conceive of such knowledge as understanding *what* artists do, *why* they do it and *how* they do it. In understanding something about expressionism, children begin to engage with the purpose of art and they can make connections with how art from this movement differs from art of other movements, cultures and religions. A varied curriculum that engages with such concepts will allow a child to understand, for example, that, in contrast to the expressionists, artists from Renaissance Italy were preoccupied with naturalism; and Chinese brush painting has traditionally been concerned with purity of form and idealised landscapes, whereas the neo-expressionists (for example, Jean-Michel Basquiat) explored how to express their feelings in a new way. Making such connections builds a solid schema from which children develop a strong understanding of the inspiring and diverse world of the history of art.

The art of looking

Building such an understanding necessitates teaching children the art of looking. Careful observation is a key skill that many artists say forms the basis of what they do. Ironically, in the multi-media age, which is so saturated with images, it is not something that we appear to be very good at. There is a current movement for 'visual literacy' being promulgated by various arts organisations (for example, the 'Superpower of Looking' primary resource promoted by Art UK[7]), which tries to promote such looking. Such a focus does not only appear in the world of education: art galleries offer 'slow art' experiences that focus on spending time looking at and discussing art (for example, Tate's 'A guide to slow looking'[8]). 'Looking' in the primary classroom might manifest itself in different ways: looking and thinking (remaining silent), looking and talking (answering both open and directed questions) and looking and drawing (looking at something to draw or looking carefully at the drawing that is being made).

Whatever mode of looking is employed, it fosters our analytical and critical faculties. Actively employing looking in the classroom emphasises the value of the looking process, the importance of which might be considered on a par with the process of creation and the outcome of that process. When paired with the explicit teaching of specialist vocabulary and the opportunity for discussion, looking promotes fluency in the expression of ideas and can be the cornerstone for sophisticated debate. For example, there is no reason why upper key stage 2 pupils should not be able to engage with and debate the ideas and opinions behind the location and ownership of objects such as the Parthenon Sculptures (commonly known as the Parthenon Marbles) or the Benin Bronzes, if they encounter a curriculum that has the ambition to engage with the objects in question.

Developing and implementing a coherent art curriculum that introduces all children to a wide range of art, that promotes the activity of looking – allowing children to engage critically with what they see – that teaches children how to use different materials with technical proficiency, and that allows them to use these materials as a mode for self-expression, is critical for social inclusion. A lack of methodical, well-sequenced instruction has its most severe effect on pupils who are socio-economically disadvantaged: a lack of art education for a pupil whose parents/carers can afford to take them to galleries, or pay for extra-curricular opportunities to draw, paint or sculpt is not going to have the same negative impact as it will for those for whom school is their only opportunity to encounter various art forms and use what they have learnt for their own expressive ends. The interrelated nature of what constitutes knowledge in art – which triangulates the historical, the conceptual and the practical – necessitates a serious, coherent and well-sequenced approach to curriculum design. Successful implementation promises rich rewards for both pupils and teachers alike.

Knowledge for all

Ben Newmark

Between about 2015 and about 2020 there was revolution in the air for English schools.

Between these years, many teachers and school leaders began challenging education orthodoxies around practice such as discovery learning and transferrable skills that had made the explicit teaching of knowledge feel somehow subversive.

Soon the fundamental importance of knowledge for learning was accepted and, all over the country, schools began rewriting schemes of work to make them 'knowledge rich'.

Then, in 2020 at an online researchED conference, Dylan Wiliam, Emeritus Professor of Educational Assessment at the UCL Institute of Education, struck a perhaps unexpectedly sober and cautionary note when he said:

> So they [curriculum developers] actually make sure there's enough stuff in the curriculum for the fastest-learning students to be occupied all year. And so there's far too much for most students.[1]

He was right – education is ultimately an expression of meritocratic social norms and the curriculum in England has almost always been developed primarily in the interests of the children who find learning easiest. That is, those children who are most likely to do well regardless of the quality of their schooling. This bias towards the already most advantaged negatively affects most other children, and can be disastrous for those who find learning hardest – those most likely to be identified as having a SEND (special educational needs and disabilities) need.

The issue begins at primary school, where children are expected to study a broad curriculum encompassing a very wide range of subjects. This is certainly good for the most able children, but may also be a reason why approximately a quarter of year 6 children don't meet what is described as the 'expected standard' in English and maths.[2] Because more time and attention are spent on a wide range of topics in a broad curriculum, the core subjects that are most important aren't covered in as much depth as they need to be for many children.

This means that many children transition to secondary school without the knowledge they need to access the curriculum there. For these children there will be no respite, as the curriculum at key stage 3 and key stage 4 is also far too big. For example, a typical GCSE history specification has nearly 300 identified teachable pieces of content. Assuming three lessons a week for 2 years – while acknowledging that in practice the available time is usually significantly less – this works out as a new piece of examinable content roughly every 20 minutes. For a student to be sure they can answer every question in their final exams they have to remember all of it, which is unrealistic for almost everyone and just absurd for some.

This increase in curriculum volume at secondary worsened post-2010, when the then-government decided to 'strengthen' GCSEs by increasing the size of specifications. This appears to have been done under the damaging misapprehension that more *stuff* meant more *challenge*, which makes just about as much sense as saying that the marathon is superior to the 100-metre sprint just because it is longer.

Key stage 4 is always the dog that wags the key stage 3 tail, and this well-intentioned but misguided drive for *more, more, more* led to a bloated key stage 3 curriculum, with most teachers across all stages now feeling that there is just too much to teach well, and aware that it is the most vulnerable children who are suffering most. Rosenshine's Principles,[3] which have been adopted by many schools in recent years as a helpful heuristic for good teaching, showcase why this is.

Rosenshine's Principles ask teachers to review previous learning daily, to present new material using small steps, to ask questions, to provide models, to guide student practice, to check for student understanding, to obtain a high success rate, to provide 'scaffolds' for difficult tasks and to supervise independent practice. How is it possible for teachers and students to do all this properly if the teacher has to move on to something brand new every 20 minutes? It isn't, and the harder a child finds learning, the more damaging being deprived of good teaching becomes for them – and the faster they lose the thread and become bewildered and lost. But there are things we can all do to address this problem.

A good place to begin would be by accepting that exposure to a dense curriculum does not in fact mean it has been learned by those subjected to it. It doesn't matter – not a bit – how impressively knowledge rich a booklet or textbook is. It doesn't matter how well sequenced, how beautifully expressed or how many likes it gets on social media. If children don't learn what's in it, then it is an indulgent and pointless waste of time. The only thing that counts is what children remember from their lessons, which is why curriculum and teaching cannot be separated.

The answer, however, is not dumbing down or downplaying the importance of knowledge. Anyone who truly believes in a knowledge-rich education needs to care about what is taught and remembered, and not what is just *planned* – unless they believe their philosophy applies to only the most able children.

Knowledge for all means knowledge for children who find learning tough, and this requires teachers and schools to be expert and judicious on what they emphasise. This is also something understood by Dylan Wiliam. In the same 2020 researchED online lecture he said 'you have to make a professional decision about what stuff you're going to leave out, and the important point here is that not all content is equally important'.[4]

Here – elegantly expressed – is the missing link between a broad, deep and challenging curriculum and accessibility and inclusion: *not all content is equally important*. This insight means that we don't actually have to throw away our dense knowledge-packed textbooks and booklets. It's important to remember that the reason we developed these was because we understood the importance of content and were turning our backs on the bankrupt idea that knowledge was merely a delivery method for so-called transferrable skills.

Now – in the interests of those children for whom learning is more of a struggle – we must go further, become even more expert, and make decisions about what is interesting, what is useful and what is essential.

A firm understanding of this allows us to organise teaching so that what's essential is prioritised in instruction, checking for understanding and formal assessment. A useful lens for doing this is to think of each topic or unit of study as having both a ceiling and a floor, and then making sure teaching prioritises the floor over the ceiling. The ceiling is what the children who find learning easiest will come away knowing. This might be everything that's in a booklet or a textbook and in the teacher's explanation and examples, which is why resources and instruction should be content rich.

The floor is the elements of knowledge that are necessary for children to access later content – those requiring mastery. The floor should have priority over the ceiling. While it may be unfortunate if the most able children don't remember everything, it doesn't stop them progressing to the next stage. Whereas if those who find learning hardest don't meet the floor standard, they are at risk of being cut off from the subsequent content.

There are already good examples of this at all stages of education. At primary school, the strong focus on phonics through carefully sequenced programmes and formalised screening checks and assessments is a way of ensuring that children have the right building blocks for learning to read well, and this has already proved successful for a great many children. More could be done, however – regrettably, in many primaries, formal phonics programmes tend to drop off at the end of year 2 because most children don't need them by that stage. While this may appear appropriately pragmatic, it is actually a very good example of 'tyranny of the majority',[5] in that it leads to the small number who do not have a firm grasp of the phonic code being unable to keep up with the rest of the class. Wise, kind and equitable primary schools would continue with their successful phonics programmes for longer (all the way to secondary school even) for those children who still need them. This would ensure that the 'floor' is in place for all children and not just some.

At secondary school, effective teaching prioritising what is essential for all children to know requires knowledgeable teachers and excellent planning. It might mean – for example – a history teacher knowing that it is far more important for a child to understand why castles have been built than it is for them to be able to reel off a wide range of design features. These features only have meaning when the reasons behind them are properly contextualised.

This approach – having a floor and ceiling in mind – might allow the school system to build on the gains made by the knowledge movement over the past 20 years, while making it more inclusive for those who find learning more difficult. It might then also help to head off accusations that a knowledge-rich curriculum is elitist or exclusive. Practically, this approach requires clarity and transparency on what is to be taught and assessed, so that all leaders, teachers and students have a shared understanding of what *all*, and not just some, children need to know.

The knowledge revolution has undoubtedly led to great progress, but there is some way to go. The logical next step is to carefully consider what in our schools' curricula is most important and how we can teach that best.

And happily, doing this would benefit all children – whether they are identified with a SEND need or not – and it would go a long way towards making our system truly inclusive.

From theory to practice: Implementing a knowledge-based secondary school curriculum for social equity

Jeremy Baker

Working at St Thomas Aquinas Catholic School in Birmingham, where half of the students are eligible for the Pupil Premium, our whole approach to curriculum development has social justice at its core. In 2017, inspired by innovative schools nationwide, we began developing our knowledge-based curriculum – a curriculum development journey that I would lead.

Energised by the incredible work of my colleagues across the sector, garnered through reading, watching recorded practice and, most importantly, visiting schools, I got to see what works. I also delved into academic research on curriculum, cognitive science and behaviour. Through all of this, I was able to find some answers to the big questions about what should be taught, how it should be taught and how it can have a disproportionately positive impact on disadvantaged students. Through the writings of Michael Young *et al* and E. D. Hirsch,[1] it became clear to me that our students have a right to, in the words of Matthew Arnold, 'the best which has been thought and said'.[2] This right is not exclusive to the wealthy or to the middle classes: it is the right of all students, including ours.

Curriculum change was needed at our school, and the work began. The curation of a knowledge-rich curriculum became central to the work of all faculty leaders in the school. We have 10 faculties, within which individual departments are housed and overseen, and our heads of faculty drove the curriculum changes at all key stages, in order to ensure that knowledge was both defined and carefully sequenced.

Building the foundation

Implementing a new curriculum begins with establishing clear principles that teachers both understand and embrace. It is impossible to achieve the commitment required to bring about change without having this shared vision.

Starting with INSET days and listening to the experiences of schools that were ahead of ours in their curriculum development journey, we had middle and senior leaders visit schools across the country that had implemented a knowledge-rich curriculum. Middle leaders, such as our heads of faculty, truly are the engine of change in schools, and they must see exemplary practice in action to understand how to drive the necessary changes. Senior leaders then facilitated significant time for our heads of faculty to make these changes a reality.

Spending time with our teachers to explain 'the why' – *why* we were implementing a knowledge-rich curriculum – was crucial to its successful implementation. At St Thomas Aquinas we talk about creating committed learners. As we implemented our curriculum, our teachers understood that to become an analytical thinker, a problem-solver or a creative individual, you must have knowledge.

With teachers liberated from the constraints of previous 'ideologies', for example project-based teaching, they were given the task of re-engaging with the foundational knowledge of their discipline. Establishing an understanding of knowledge categories and debating what should be taught – and more contentiously, what should be left out – was crucial to this.

Fundamental to the implementation of our knowledge-rich curriculum has been an effective professional development model. Giving dedicated time every Wednesday afternoon to training, and ensuring that the majority of this time is under the direction of the teachers' head of faculty, has been a cornerstone of our work. This professional development model allows for a disciplinary angle so that the head of modern foreign languages, for example, can prioritise phonics, while the science leader can focus on how to use subject booklets effectively to drive improvement.

In addition to this, we have also invested in some world-class training, by inviting teaching experts Doug Lemov and Alex Quigley to talk to our staff about topics such as building belonging in a school and aspects of literacy. Integrating the knowledge acquired from these sessions into our common framework for learning and professional development curriculum ensures that this work lasts far into the future, and doesn't just disappear like the INSETs of old. The danger of new teachers joining a system they don't fully understand presents challenges for both the incoming teachers themselves and the school subject leaders. Professional development must constantly evolve to help bridge this gap.

Also central to the implementation of our knowledge-rich curriculum is explicit instruction.[3] And, significantly, we have not found convincing teachers about the merits of explicit instruction to prove too difficult. Most people I have worked with know that we need to convey knowledge within carefully organised schema; that is, through a framework that helps our brains to organise and interpret information. And finding core models with which to connect this thinking helps staff to apply it to their practice. For example, using cognitive neuroscientific researcher Efrat Furst's network model[4] to enhance our understanding and application of schema theory has proved critical to building teacher knowledge. In a nutshell, Efrat Furst's model explains how knowledge is stored and represented in the brain through interconnected neuronal patterns or networks. It highlights the dynamic nature of these networks, which are initially created during learning and then stored in long-term memory. By leveraging this model, teachers have restructured what they teach to reflect the principle that knowledge is 'sticky': sequence is critical because students need to connect new learning to their existing knowledge. And as teachers, it is our job to make the links between facts explicit to our students: this is where *understanding* lies. Ultimately, the outcome of this work is that the curriculum is more coherent, and as a result students learn more.

Whilst these curriculum and teaching developments have been critical to our school's success, for students to learn there must also be clear rules and consequences, underpinned by a culture of love and care. As such, alongside our curriculum thinking we also made significant changes to our behaviour policy, including extensive work on building a strong sense of belonging for students. We believe that excellent behaviour is the foundation of a knowledge-based approach. Without it, students can't sit and listen to the expert in the room, the teacher; they don't have the discipline to transition to and from a 'turn and talk'; and they don't come equipped with the necessary study materials to allow them to succeed. A centralised and well-implemented behaviour system enables all students to achieve because it allows teachers to focus on *teaching*.

Curriculum content and implementation

We do unapologetically teach facts at St Thomas Aquinas. Facts liberate us – they allow us to think, to produce works of art, to be moved by literature and to speak new languages. But at the heart of this approach is of course the crucial question of which facts and what knowledge? The Ofsted subject reports[5] have provided some direction to this discussion, but when we began developing our knowledge-rich curriculum such guidance didn't exist. Instead, we used our connections with subject associations, universities and existing literature to help formulate our thinking. Our English faculty, for example, inspired by thinking from the University of Birmingham, organised their curriculum into epochs, to enable students to develop a deeper understanding of literature. The English faculty was also influenced by the writing of Michael Young *et al*, which emphasised the social construction of knowledge and the importance of understanding the context in which powerful knowledge is produced.[6] Our students therefore now begin, in year 7, at the start of the Classical period of ancient Greece. Our year 7s focus on classical tragedy, learning the famous myths and legends of King Midas and Pandora's box, and all the while expanding not only their language and structural analysis skills but also their critical-thinking skills and their ability to evaluate texts with their own thoughts and interpretations. Year 7 students then continue through to the Medieval period, studying the concept of the Medieval morality play. They then move on to the Renaissance, focusing on humanity's relationship with nature, ending this historical journey in the Enlightenment era where they, much like the freethinkers themselves, are stretched to thoroughly question the texts.

Following our discussions on knowledge, we spent a long time ensuring the application of key principles from within cognitive science. We have certainly learned that the most successful faculties within the school don't do anything other than double down on what works, and do so consistently, day in day out. We have found consistency to be king when it comes to making changes across a school.

Faculties such as PE have seen significant improvements in their outcomes because they do those elements core to a knowledge-rich approach well. The routine testing of knowledge in PE ensures information is stored in students' long-term memories. Deliberately practising writing with students within PE, for example, accelerates students' learning; students are explicitly taught how to write in multi-clausal sentences, improving their analysis of sporting performance. The PE faculty have fully engaged with our professional enquiry programme, which gives time to all teachers to read research papers, watch each other teach, reflect on their experiences and write everything up into a coherent and reflective document that moves practice forward in their faculty.

Overcoming obstacles: Lessons learned
A 'theory of change'[7] underpins our thinking about implementation, but even when using so-called 'best bets', cognitive science and a commitment to the belief that knowledge is the key to thinking, there are always challenges and mistakes. Overemphasising the role of knowledge organisers is one such error that we made in the early days of our curriculum work. Knowledge organisers became synonymous with a knowledge-based approach, and whilst they did facilitate great discussions about the knowledge that should be included in our curriculum, in reality they

are more valuable for some subjects or lessons than others. Ultimately, the emphasis needs to be about mastery and a commitment to learn core knowledge; distilling this into a single sheet of paper can distort the curriculum into a short list of facts that students then perceive to be a revision guide.

Like knowledge organisers, teacher-produced booklets also proliferated at our school; however, schools should be cautious about adopting them. At their best, teacher-produced booklets are professionally produced and carefully structured, and enable consistency with the principles established in your school. Producing good knowledge organisers also needs to be done very carefully across the disciplines, and takes time. Instead of seeking to 'reinvent the wheel', there are some excellent textbooks in some subject areas, and I do feel that we can do more as a sector to share resources in this format for the benefit of all.

Running training on literacy has been another intrinsic aspect of our knowledge-rich curriculum development work, and we are now in the sixth year of an implementation plan that is continuing indefinitely. Working with a staff body among whom many were not formally educated in the intricacies of English grammar presents challenges for leaders attempting to teach writing. Using expertise within the school, therefore, we worked slowly through a professional development writing curriculum with our staff. We explicitly teach our students to write in multi-clausal sentences, building up from basic sentence construction activities to sentence expanding with appositives, relative clauses and embedded clauses. Taking a disciplinary approach to writing, therefore, we give our staff time to *understand* the tools in order to apply them to their lessons. The clear outcome is that students are more able to express their ideas and connect knowledge strands together to demonstrate their understanding.

And finally, a note on assessing our knowledge-rich curriculum. Some may see it as liberating that we have been freed up from national accountability measures at key stage 3 – and I would indeed be one of them. However, a consequence of this is that schools have found it increasingly difficult to communicate attainment and progress between years 7 and 10. We have tried grades, bands, raw marks and a system that attempts to assess the proportion of the curriculum that has been learned. All these trialled systems have had their issues, and I write this today happy with the raw mark system we use but very open about the weaknesses that are inherent within it. Raw marks allow us to see the nuances in achievement on a test, and to focus on what has or has not been learned. The ongoing weakness within this assessment approach, however, is that it is not yet a model that establishes progression in each subject.

The outcomes that drive us

With a seemingly constant call from students for more critical thinking and a 'relevant' curriculum, the challenge for us is to persuade teachers, leaders and policymakers that the route to lifelong learning starts with *knowing*. Reducing a curriculum to a student's interests may have short-term benefits, but to deny them the knowledge they need to engage in the full conversation of life is to do a generation of children a disservice.

Our experience at St Thomas Aquinas demonstrates that implementing a knowledge-based curriculum requires more than just theoretical understanding – it demands practical wisdom, consistent application and an unwavering commitment to social justice. It has resulted in a significant improvement to our exam results, but even more significantly, our students now leave as committed learners,

learners who go out into the world to make it a better place. Our students are able to approach new challenges and engage with the critical thinking they will need to succeed in the future, because they have the foundation of core knowledge that active global citizens require in the 21st century. In championing knowledge for all, we strive not only to educate, but also to equalise.

Teaching a knowledge-rich secondary history curriculum

Harry Hudson

The critical caricature

For some, the concept of a knowledge-rich approach to teaching history instantly evokes austere 19th century schoolrooms and Thomas Gradgrind in Dickens' *Hard Times*: 'Now, what I want is, Facts. Teach these boys and girls nothing but Facts. Facts alone are wanted in life. Plant nothing else, and root out everything else.'[1] In this imagining, the 21st century knowledge-rich approach is simply Gradgrindianism reheated, a modern take on the high-Victorian fetish for facts.

For others, knowledge-rich is redolent of a perceived public-school tradition of teaching history – tweedy Eton masters giving eccentric lectures, waxing lyrical about the great deeds of great men. By this reckoning, a knowledge-rich approach has a whiff of privilege and nostalgia, a desire to recall the simpler and less contested truths of simpler and less contested times.

And history, it seems, is particularly vulnerable to this sort of characterisation. Maybe this has something to do with the intrinsic nature of studying the past. The need to learn dates, for example, lingers long in the memory of many past students of history. 'I was useless at history at school myself', goes the not uncommon refrain from parents across the desk at parents' evenings. 'I could just never learn the dates.'

Maybe it's because of an awareness of the sheer immensity of the past, the vast amount of material waiting to be tackled. Seen in this light, the study of history seems to be an almost impossible task – and one that the knowledge-rich approach appears to respond to with a desperate attempt to cram as many facts as possible into the too-little time available.

The power of a knowledge-rich approach

Whatever the reasons for this caricature, it remains precisely that – a caricature, built upon many of the usual half-truths common to caricatures. It should hardly need stating that no teacher advocating a knowledge-rich approach imagines himself or herself to be a latter-day Gradgrind, any more than they want to serve up an unrelenting diet of miserably rote-learnt facts.

On the contrary, those who advocate a knowledge-rich approach do so precisely because it allows the past to come to life. The principle that lies at the heart of the approach – that the acquisition of knowledge should be seen as an end in itself, rather than just as a stepping-stone to other aims – gets about as far away as is possible from reducing history to a litany of unmemorable events. Indeed, to see it simply as a fact-centred approach to teaching history is to miss the point: it's a *history*-centred approach to teaching history, giving history the space it needs to speak on its own terms.

This gives the study of history an exhilarating vitality. By putting the knowledge unapologetically front and centre, it explicitly tells pupils that the stories and characters of the past deserve to be taught for their own inherent interest. A knowledge-rich history curriculum allows pupils to explore the vagaries of human nature and to appreciate how they have affected the course of history; this, in turn, enables pupils to pick up echoes of the past in the present.

It understands too that the practice of *'doing* history' – analysing source material, evaluating historians' interpretations of the past and building one's own – relies upon a strong foundation of carefully taught knowledge. To fully appreciate how the past is contested and fought over, you need to get to grips with the actual stuff of the past first.

And perhaps most importantly, precisely by taking this knowledge-rich approach, history is made memorable and becomes more likely to stick in pupils' memories in the long term. This of course requires that those designing a curriculum – typically, but not solely, heads of department – think deeply about the specific detail of what's going to be taught and in what order, so that the curriculum they create allows its various parts to complement and reinforce each other. It's also important that curriculum designers then make this thinking explicit to all those who will actually teach the curriculum, so that they too fully understand the rationale behind it in order to teach it more effectively.

But when this happens, they can realise a curriculum that pupils both enjoy and remember – a knowledge-rich approach doesn't enervate the past, it empowers it.

Challenges facing a knowledge-rich approach

The caricature of the knowledge-rich approach doesn't, however, come from nowhere. As so often with caricatures, it does flag up some genuine challenges that can't simply be dismissed. If history shows us anything, it's that uncritical advocacy for a cause tends to end badly.

Several of the fears surrounding a knowledge-rich approach to teaching history are, to varying degrees, justified – there is absolutely the potential for it to go wrong, and it does. The challenge for advocates of the knowledge-rich approach is to know how to respond to these possible pitfalls.

1. Does a knowledge-rich history curriculum make for boring lessons?

One of the most recurrent challenges levelled against knowledge-rich history lessons – or, perhaps more accurately, against the concept of knowledge-rich history lessons – is that they are dry and boring. It is feared that pupils become too passive, and that teachers simply lecture to them: education becomes something done *to* pupils.

There are several responses to this. First, it is true that knowledge-rich lessons are indeed typically much simpler than those of other approaches. However, rather than leading to dull lessons, this relative simplicity is one of the approach's great benefits.

The knowledge-rich history lesson contrasts starkly with the task-driven lesson so characteristic of the 1990s and 2000s, in which pupils are required to spend more time thinking about the logistics of tasks than the actual material they are meant to be learning: fiddly card-sorts, cutting and sticking, oversized posters, puppet shows, make-your-own plasticine desk sculptures, 'work stations' in different parts of the room.

While these might provide pupils with a quick, sugar-rush thrill of activity, they do not offer the sort of diet that can sustain their interest in the long term. Teachers therefore often find that these types of tasks quickly lose their lustre – and pupils' interest. Sustaining that interest really only comes when they are able to engage meaningfully with the history they are meant to be studying.

In contrast to a task-driven lesson, a typical knowledge-rich history lesson might revolve around a teacher reading through a text with their class. The teacher and pupils might take it in turns to read aloud, and the teacher might supplement the text with their own explanations, clarifying difficult concepts, defining tricky words, and bringing out the interest of what is being taught. They would likely support this approach with carefully chosen images, maps and diagrams on a set of slides.

The teacher would intersperse the reading and explanation with oral questioning of pupils, both to check their understanding, and to encourage them to think beyond the text itself. Why might this have happened? What might be the consequence of that? How does this link to what was studied last week? Pupils might also periodically do some writing in their books, either some short-answer questions or a piece of more extended writing.

The simplicity of this format is not a drawback but a strength, as it means that the history is allowed to take centre stage, unencumbered by procedural fluff. Far from producing dull lessons, it allows for dynamic lessons that zing with energy, as enthusiastic and skilled teachers are able to bring the material to life and allow the past to sing.

Enthusiasm is infectious, and pupils are far more likely to be drawn into the wonderful and varied worlds of the past by teachers who are themselves unashamedly captivated by the stories they are telling. This builds a virtuous circle, when pupils respond with corresponding enthusiasm, which in turns serves to feed that of their teachers. These lessons hum with life.

However, it's true that as a format, a knowledge-rich history lesson also has the potential to come unstuck. This is particularly the case if the teacher, especially one new to a knowledge-rich approach, falls into thinking that the very fact of teaching in this way means that the history will *automatically* come alive and that their classes will, by default, be captivated by their every word.

Similarly, the obvious emphasis that a knowledge-rich approach places on 'the knowledge' means that it can be tempting for teachers to kid themselves into thinking that their own grasp and love of the subject matter means that their lessons could never be boring. If they find the material interesting, surely their pupils will too.

If only it was this simple. The knowledge-rich approach has many strengths, but it is not simply a plug-and-go panacea. Although a knowledge-rich history curriculum puts in place the conditions for more engaging and effective lessons, those lessons don't just teach themselves, and it doesn't reduce the need for the teacher to put real thought into the planning of their lessons – indeed, if anything, it increases it.

It would certainly be to misunderstand knowledge-rich lessons to imagine that they require any less of the teacher than alternative approaches. On the contrary, the teacher's skill is never more to the fore than in a knowledge-rich lesson, as they need to use all of their craft to bring the material to life. While in many ways this can therefore demand more of the teacher – in both the planning and execution of the lesson – the key is to ensure that teachers receive proper training in how to teach effective knowledge-rich lessons.

A novice teacher of knowledge-rich history might therefore be encouraged to consider what features of the lesson they are going to particularly emphasise to bring it to life; what questions they are going to ask; what they can predict pupils will struggle with; and how they are going to take into account and respond to the varying levels of prior knowledge that pupils will bring to the lesson. Careful mentoring can help with all of these, and indeed is essential to anyone starting out with the knowledge-rich approach.

In short, there is nothing intrinsically dry, repetitive or boring about a knowledge-rich history lesson. Rather, because it gives so much space to the history itself, it is designed precisely to allow lessons to have maximum life. This does, however, require well-trained, knowledgeable, enthusiastic and skilled teachers. A poorly implemented knowledge-rich history lesson can indeed be dry, repetitive or boring – but then that is true of any lesson, regardless of the approach behind it.

2. Does knowledge come at the expense of skills in a knowledge-rich history curriculum?

Another criticism levelled at the knowledge-rich approach is that its focus on knowledge too often comes at the expense of skills. And indeed, it is easy to see how you could think that an approach to history teaching explicitly labelled 'knowledge rich' might place less value on teaching historical skills. However, to view the knowledge-rich approach as being somehow antagonistic towards teaching skills is to set up a false dichotomy.

All history teachers, including those taking a knowledge-rich approach, want their pupils to be able to analyse a primary source, evaluate an historical interpretation and work with second-order historical concepts, such as significance, cause, consequence, change and continuity. All history teachers recognise that these are essential components of what it means to learn about history as a discipline, while, more prosaically, they also all know that their pupils' GCSE and A level grades will require these skills. It is therefore not a case of either/or, but rather both/and.

Moreover, to draw a binary distinction between knowledge and skills is really to misconceive what skills are. Skills cannot be taught in the abstract and can only emerge from a strong fundament of knowledge. Being asked to 'analyse' an Elizabethan portrait, for example, in a year 7 lesson on the Tudors, requires a significant amount of knowledge about the second half of the 16th century. Knowledge and skills don't merely co-exist, but are mutually dependent.

It's worth adding here that the skills a history teacher would want to teach their pupils are often different from those of teachers of other subjects. An explanation in history is different from an explanation in science, for example – where the former typically gives a much greater role to interpretation, the latter is more concerned with using empirical evidence and experimentation. Similarly, you would approach the analysis of a First World War poem from different perspectives in a history lesson and an English lesson.

This point on context matters because it highlights another of the challenges facing a knowledge-rich teacher of any subject: how to make sure that you aren't blindly adopting techniques and methods that aren't specifically suited to your subject. This is something that history teachers have to be alive to as they implement a knowledge-rich curriculum: where a certain type of knowledge organiser (a document that summarises key facts about a topic, often on one page) might work well in science, for instance, it might have to be designed very differently in history to be effective.

3. Can there be too much knowledge?
Finally, perhaps the greatest challenge for a knowledge-rich history curriculum is one that confronts the teacher before they have even entered the classroom, namely the risk of filling the curriculum with *too much* knowledge. Anathema though it may seem to an advocate of a knowledge-rich approach, there *can* be too much of a good thing.

The current history specifications at GCSE are a case in point. Here, an understandable desire to expose children to as much knowledge as possible has been allowed to spill over to excess. The amount of material that GCSE pupils are expected to learn is too large, and as a result, fascinating history can end up being reduced to mere 'content' that has to be 'got through' as quickly as possible.

Knowing when enough is enough is therefore one of the greatest challenges for the knowledge-rich approach to history. As classroom teachers, we are limited in our ability to do anything about this at key stages 4 and 5, where GCSE and A level curricula are ultimately determined by exam boards. However, it's something we are much more able to act upon at key stage 3, where schools have greater autonomy to design their own curricula.

This opportunity at key stage 3 precisely enables the sense of ownership and empowerment for classroom teachers so fundamental to the success of a knowledge-rich curriculum. For knowledge-rich really to work, teachers need to buy into the curriculum choices that have been made, and this can only really happen when they are able to build the curriculum for themselves.

This is both a challenge and an opportunity for those with curriculum responsibilities. It is a challenge to ensure that there *is* a sense of shared ownership of a curriculum even among those members of a department who might not have taken an active part in writing it, but also an opportunity to draw upon multiple colleagues' expertise when developing existing curricula.

And when everything comes together …

When it is planned carefully and then taught well, the knowledge-rich approach is an incredibly powerful way of teaching history. It is of course important for advocates of a knowledge-rich curriculum to be aware of its challenges and then take the steps necessary to address them. But if they do, they are empowered to teach lessons that open their pupils' eyes to the wonders of history, in all its awesome colour.

The implementation of a knowledge-rich secondary science curriculum: Our journey

Jason Molloy

Establishing primary principles

The development of our knowledge-rich science curriculum originated with a small team of experienced science teachers in a small secondary school in the Leicestershire countryside. By way of context, our school resources are below standard compared to your average secondary science department: a couple of science labs between 800 students and limited equipment and technology. A combination that could seem challenging when trying to break away from the status quo of the secondary science curriculum, but in reality the limitation of our resources played to our advantage. With limited access to ICT, labs and equipment, we were required to deliver a rich curriculum with little more than pen and paper as resources. At the time of designing our knowledge-rich science curriculum, the school had recently transitioned from a middle school (years 7–9) into a full secondary school (going up to year 11). The existing curriculum was therefore very much in its infancy at that stage.

My team were presented with a unique opportunity to critique and challenge the flaws in the way secondary science had previously been taught, and to enrich the curriculum beyond the current GCSE specifications. The opportunity to focus on a knowledge-rich curriculum was exciting but also daunting, not just in terms of the scale of the task but also the complexity of such a project.

Frustrations with our existing practice

The frustrations my team had, prior to implementing a knowledge-rich curriculum, ranged from the time and effort it took to plan individual lessons to the onerous task of marking books; the latter often leading to out-of-date and therefore ineffective feedback to students. But our biggest frustration was that students failed to remember key facts and information over an extended period of time, which made recall extremely difficult towards year 11, and the *application* of knowledge virtually impossible. When it came to science practicals, students lacked the knowledge to understand what they were actually doing – they were unfamiliar with the scientific method and how the practical supported their learning. The learning experience was one of cognitive overload. Students had to process listening to the teacher, transcribe notes from the board and memorise new information. As it stood, the curriculum presented learning inconsistencies within year groups, un-sequenced lessons and topics, and delayed feedback from marking.

There were also further frustrations about what was not working well. For those in a leadership role, the quality assurance process of ensuring consistency and high standards within lessons was difficult to monitor, and providing feedback that could be applied in order to improve the teachers' practice was absent.

Curriculum design

Asking what was wrong with our current practice was the first step to eventually realising that a knowledge-rich curriculum solved many of our issues. There wasn't then a single starting point to the design of our science knowledge-rich curriculum – in fact many strands of the curriculum design set off in unison.

Once our initial discussions to identify common misconceptions (for example about latest scientific terminology) and frustrations with the current curriculum had been crystallised, we developed a series of primary principles to foster integrity across the science curriculum. These principles were: to teach the best that's thought and said; that teachers should work smarter not harder; and that students should experience a science curriculum that stretches beyond GCSE, regardless of their aspirations in life. The sequence of our curriculum was based upon identifying the prerequisites for each of the topics we wanted to teach. For example, previously, in year 7 students were taught a few lessons on acids and alkalis and the pH scale. In summary, how we use a universal indicator to identify if a substance is an acid or an alkali from the colours on the pH scale. By the end of these lessons, could the students tell you what acids and alkalis actually are, and what the pH scale represents? No. So we asked 'What are the prerequisites for teaching the pH scale?'. Students would need to know about: concentration, logarithmic scale, a hydrogen ion, formation of ions, bonding, atomic structure, electrostatic charges and so on. Secure knowledge of previous topics was essential: therefore, each major topic that we thought should be included in the curriculum was front-loaded with teaching the prerequisites in a sequenced order. This sequencing process determined the curriculum: for everything you wanted to teach, you needed to ask 'What do students need to know first?'.

Once our topics had been mapped out, the logical step was to find the common denominator for each – this became the sequence of our science curriculum. We realised that the fundamental concept of energy should be the origin of our curriculum, as everything ultimately led back to this. Before moving on to anything in biology, knowledge and understanding of the chemical world was essential. So, we moved there next. Molecules needed to be taught before digestion: how would the students know what enzymes, carbohydrates, lipids and proteins are if they didn't know what a molecule is?

Sequencing of the topics was vital to the success of the curriculum, and we needed to ensure that this was not compromised. But we also had to recognise that the curriculum is non-linear. Instead, it took on the appearance of an inverted spiral pyramid, with topics being revisited in the latter years, but in greater depth and complexity. In other words, the fundamental knowledge is secured in the early stages and is then synoptically revisited over 5 years.

I remember trying to proudly summarise our science curriculum development to a non-teacher friend of mine, saying 'We basically organised what we were going to teach from the simple science to the more complex, then made sure that the students remembered the important information before moving onto the next topic, and then secured this knowledge in long-term memory so they could apply it in unfamiliar situations in the future.' His response: 'I thought that's what teachers always did?'.

Implementation

At Saint Martin's, we hit the rising crest of the knowledge-rich curriculum wave at a time when knowledge organisers became *in vogue*. We duly created and published our own versions, which was a logical starting point: when mapping such a behemoth task, these knowledge organisers created a blueprint to sequence our lessons within each topic. A finer method of planning was required using the same principles of sequencing we used for our topics – the prerequisites – but now it was by the minute, not week by week.

The knowledge organisers alone were not a silver bullet: they had to be complemented with something else that could undo the weaknesses we identified early on. Our resources had to improve, and the available textbooks were not of a challenging enough standard for what we wanted to deliver.

I also didn't want teachers to write all their own lessons individually. It was time to say goodbye to the days of a non-specialist working twice as hard as the subject expert next door, and only to deliver a comparatively weaker lesson. Who loses out in that scenario? Both the teacher and the students. To avoid this science timetable lottery, I wanted to deploy teachers to work within their specialisms. I wanted them to become excited, passionate and stimulated about their subject. I wanted them to rekindle their reasons for studying their subject at A level and university. Secondary to that, I wanted improved consistency in terms of content across the department – trust the subject expert to write the lesson content, trust the teachers to execute it to their classes. I wanted feedback on lessons to be focused on teaching, not content; this had more impact and value and could be implemented immediately in future lessons and have a high impact. My challenge was to develop a team of teachers who enjoyed putting together the best their subject has to offer (people, discoveries, failures, successes, stories), to then share it with young people in the hope of passing on this enthusiasm, awe and wonder.

Our tool for delivering such content was a knowledge book. A knowledge book is essentially a 'working' textbook, and it replaced the typical exercise book that our students previously used to make notes. Within these knowledge books, the required knowledge is printed for the students to read, along with recall and application questions and additional resources, such as activity sheets and extended response activities.

There were a few available knowledge books knocking around at other schools, but they were in the embryonic stages, and they were tailored for each individual school setting. In contrast to some other schools, we had excellent behaviour, high standards and routine; students walked into the classroom ready to learn, so we had a head start already. To solidify the behaviour culture, we created a standardised start to every lesson: nothing complicated, no bells and whistles. The question was 'How do you start a lesson with just a black pen?'; the answer was, ask the students some questions about what they learned previously and make sure they have the resources to do this from the moment they enter the room.

Our knowledge books were therefore tailor-made to our environment, and they fundamentally provided the right balance of retrieval, knowledge, application and challenge that we wanted. They allowed the teachers to focus on delivery and not on planning content, they were written by subject experts and, most importantly, they reduced the cognitive load for the students in lessons. Students could be asked to put their pens down and focus on the teacher at the front of the room, knowing that accurate knowledge and information was already printed in their books; all they needed to do was make annotations and notes along the way. The knowledge books evolved over several years. They became less prescriptive about how lessons would be delivered and instead offered students the security of receiving a written version of accurate knowledge from the lesson, allowing the teacher a better opportunity to deploy the right teaching strategies for their specific audience.

Secondary principles

Over time, secondary principles revealed themselves during the design and implementation of our knowledge-rich curriculum. We identified that we wanted to raise the minimum standard, and to ensure that all students should have the opportunity to study science beyond GCSE even if their future pathway looked potentially unrelated. We wanted our students to access the same level and quality of curriculum as a first-rate fee-paying school and to raise their aspirations in our subjects. We wanted equal opportunity for all, regardless of student background or any additional needs they may have.

Misconceptions about a knowledge-rich curriculum

The image of a knowledge-rich lesson to an 'outsider' might be very bleak: students sitting in silence, teachers preaching from the front of the room in a cold and dull manner. However, this picture couldn't be further from the truth for our lessons. We have welcomed hundreds of visitors to our science department who walk into vibrant, engaging, energetic and passionate lessons, with high levels of student participation and dialogue between teachers and students. Our students have excellent subject knowledge and recall facts swiftly, not to become walking encyclopaedias, but so that they can answer and ask questions with clarity and precision. Teacher explanations don't need layers upon layers of 'pre-teaching' and reminders of key vocabulary – instead, in our classrooms, everyone talks like a scientist!

The security of delivering a knowledge-rich curriculum, and the resources to complement it, provide the teacher at the front of the classroom with an audience of attentive students. This is because the students know what the teacher is talking about. And this is because the students have stored the key facts and information in their long-term memory so that more challenging and complex explanations can follow without having to constantly review the definition of a key term. The bank of knowledge that students bring into the classroom is the key to unlocking its application, which in science is what we strive to achieve. Underpinning these great lessons is an accomplished teacher with an arsenal of teaching strategies to carefully implement with the young minds they have in front of them.

The notion of a knowledge-rich science curriculum can often give the impression that it's deficient in practical work. And isn't science about learning skills by doing experiments? Yes, but instead of light-touch, time-consuming practical experiences (with students showing great participation but very little understanding of why they are performing an activity), our practical lessons have been designed to make sure they support the curriculum and allow the fundamental scientific enquiry skills to be honed. Our students are taught to follow the scientific method, ask questions about the world around them, analyse data and draw conclusions. They become problem-solvers and critical-thinkers, and they learn to explain their decisions. We develop curious and inquisitive minds, and all built on strong foundations of knowledge. Ultimately, therefore, our students can explain what they think with accurate language, describing trends and extrapolating from data and drawing conclusions, to then be able to explain whether their hypothesis is supported by the evidence.

Outcomes

Arguably the litmus test for our science knowledge-rich curriculum is in our results, which have been consistently positive over the past 5 years. However, perhaps the ultimate litmus test is that when we have visitors, the biggest sceptics of a knowledge-rich curriculum often leave our school with a very different opinion about how it actually works in the classroom. Many of our visitors are reassured when they see great teaching and learning, *not* dictation and recital. They walk away inspired by what they witness and want to delve deeper into the development, implementation and impact of the curriculum.

Implementing a knowledge-rich curriculum in a special needs school

Kasia Glinka and Rebecca Ryman

Maplewell Hall School, a maintained special school in Leicestershire, serves students aged 11–19 with cognition and learning needs, communication and interaction challenges, social, emotional and mental health (SEMH) issues, and sensory impairments. All 321 students have an Education, Health and Care Plan (EHCP), and students may be admitted at any point during their school career. Over the past 2 years, there has been a significant shift in the student profile, with an increasing number of students with SEMH and complex needs.

'Knowledge is power': never has this statement held more weight than when it comes to the most vulnerable individuals in our society.

The implementation of a knowledge-rich curriculum has marked a fundamental shift in educational practice at Maplewell, driven by our students' rising levels of attainment and our belief in their ability to achieve even more highly.

Our concept of a knowledge-rich curriculum is rooted in the belief that all students, regardless of any additional needs, deserve access to a broad and deep education that prepares them for success both in and beyond school, nurturing a strong sense of self-belief and an ability to engage with the wider world.

The need for change was clear when outcomes and observations confirmed that a consistent barrier to learning for the majority of our students (and therefore a barrier to them achieving their full potential) was retention of key knowledge, which was not improving as rapidly as we had hoped with the curriculum model and pedagogical methods we had in place. We therefore explored the details of Ofsted's 2019 research overview of the evidence underpinning their education inspection framework,[1] as well as their subsequent subject reviews, which emphasised the importance of a knowledge-rich curriculum.[2] However, we knew that for our setting, the concept would require adaptations. As highlighted in Labour's 2022 report on learning and skills:

> There should be no conflict between a knowledge rich curriculum, and a broad and innovative framework which develops the analytical, creative, and therefore entrepreneurial mindset of the employees of the future.[3]

Our adaptations needed to ensure that students developed not only a strong foundation of knowledge but also the cognitive, social and practical skills necessary for success beyond school.

Our adaptation of a knowledge-rich curriculum model was shaped by philosopher and educator Paulo Freire's critique of the traditional 'banking model of education', where students passively receive information.[4] For us, this aligned with the issues our students faced when teachers attempted to impart the amount of content required to sit higher level qualifications – for example, GCSEs in English literature or triple science. We began to further explore Paulo Freire's concept of 'problem-posing' education, in which students actively engage with knowledge, ask questions and develop critical-thinking skills.[5] Through this research, we concluded that a successful knowledge-rich curriculum is neither about merely absorbing disconnected facts, nor about focusing solely on life skills. Rather, it provides structured and meaningful content that enables young people to critically engage with the world. By fostering active inquiry instead of passive reception, an adapted knowledge-rich curriculum model can equip special educational needs and disabilities (SEND) students with essential cognitive tools, preparing them for a broad range of academic and life experiences.

The success of our knowledge-rich curriculum for Maplewell students is clear, both in our data and anecdotally. The percentage of students attaining GCSE grades 4–9 has risen significantly, from 21 per cent in 2023 to 32 per cent in 2024. Our students have reported that this curriculum rich in knowledge and cultural capital has allowed them to find common ground with peers when entering mainstream colleges post-16. Returning from a college visit, one of our students excitedly told us how he had 'bonded' with mainstream students over the GCSE English literature Macbeth question; he felt that, no matter his journey, he was on a level with students who had accessed a mainstream education.

Curriculum design for knowledge retention

The knowledge-rich curriculum at Maplewell is designed to be inclusive, ensuring that all students have equal access to academic content. Research from cognitive science shows that background knowledge plays a pivotal role in reading comprehension and overall learning.[6] Thus, our curriculum ensures that all students – no matter their background or individual needs – can access and retain the knowledge that is critical to their future success.

In practice, we combine knowledge with skill development, ensuring that students not only acquire facts but also build the cognitive tools needed to analyse, question and apply what they learn. For example, in English, students are exposed to a diverse range of literature, challenging stereotypes and expanding their perspectives. In science, students engage with theories and concepts that they can apply to real-world situations, fostering both understanding and practical knowledge.

Underpinning this, in order to improve literacy and reading comprehension (which are essential for our students' academic success) we have implemented a daily reading curriculum, offering a personalised approach for different reading ages. Through a daily 35-minute tutor time dedicated to reading, including targeted interventions, we focus on giving students the reading skills and knowledge they need to engage with all aspects of the curriculum. Our students accessing these targeted interventions make on average 18 months' progress in their reading age in a year; this rapid progress allows them to access all areas of the curriculum confidently.

Implementation of a knowledge-rich curriculum

Our first steps towards implementing a knowledge-rich curriculum began with asking our core curriculum leads to map key knowledge. Initially, we asked them to pinpoint exactly what they want our students to finish each year *knowing*; for example, what a metaphor is and what it does. The concept of 'powerful knowledge' is a useful term when attempting to narrow down vast amounts of content.[7] Beginning with core subjects allowed our expert subject teachers to provide valuable support to foundation subject leads in creating explicit, well-structured curriculum plans.

We then explored how knowledge was categorised, to further narrow down exactly what we wanted our students to know – and crucially, *why* we wanted them to know that information above all else. We asked our curriculum leads to separate the core knowledge from the hinterland knowledge; this hinterland knowledge helps our students explore and apply their knowledge, but it is not the focus for retention.

Creating interdisciplinary links formed the next phase. This connected approach helped reinforce and deepen students' understanding across subjects, allowing shared approaches and methods to be embedded across different subjects.

Foundation subject teachers also recognised the need to adapt their pedagogical approaches to ensure that all students could access and engage with challenging content. We asked subject leaders to work with the curriculum leads to break down the content into smaller, manageable chunks that align with the sequence. Alongside this, we asked them to plan how new content connects with prior knowledge and how it can be revisited at later stages of learning for consolidation. Refining lesson planning and encouraging students to evaluate concepts facilitates a deeper acquisition of knowledge, ensuring that each lesson builds upon the knowledge gained in earlier stages and that students' understanding deepens over time. For example, we might see the English curriculum explicitly teach metaphors in year 7, progressing to more complex figurative language analysis in year 9.

Inclusivity: The role of assessment

Assessment plays a central role in Maplewell's knowledge-rich curriculum by systematically measuring how effectively students are acquiring, retaining and applying core knowledge. The role of assessment has evolved alongside the curriculum, shifting from a sole focus on immediate understanding to also tracking long-term retention and meaningful application of knowledge. A bespoke adaptation of our tracking platform allows us to track the progress of individuals, ensuring all students progress at their own pace. Continuous formative assessments help our teachers to adjust lessons, allowing gaps in knowledge to be addressed early.

In addition to summative assessments (testing understanding of a component of learning and preparing students for external examinations), we introduced low-stakes 'knowledge checks' planned for key interim points within each subject. These may take the form of a set of short-answer questions or a vocabulary quiz, for example, and inform teachers as to whether students are retaining the knowledge we expected prior to a summative assessment. This allows for continuous development of the curriculum and pedagogical strategies to support progress.

When introducing performance analysis tools – such as CAT4 (cognitive ability testing), FFT Aspire (progress benchmarking) and NGRT (reading attainment) – we set high standards for all students. These standardised assessments provide objective data to identify strengths, gaps and barriers to achievement, ensuring that targeted support can be implemented effectively. For students with additional needs, whose primary school level educational data may be limited or insufficient, these tools support staff in tracking individual and group performance and setting high-expectation targets aligned with national benchmarks. Additionally, the NGRT assessment focuses on reading comprehension and fluency, providing valuable insights into the literacy levels of SEND students and enabling targeted interventions.

Challenges and obstacles

Criticism of knowledge-rich curricula in educational discourse broadly falls into two categories: first, that they prioritise knowledge at the expense of skills, and second, that they can be overly prescriptive, limiting teacher autonomy and flexibility. Our approach seeks to challenge these perceptions by ensuring that knowledge acquisition is deeply embedded alongside skills development, and that subject leaders retain the flexibility to adapt content to meet students' diverse needs. Nevertheless, the implementation of a knowledge-rich curriculum at Maplewell has not been without its challenges. Some of our teachers were initially sceptical, particularly those concerned that the curriculum might overlook the importance of life skills or overwhelm students with academic demands. However, through consistent professional development, positive student outcomes and regular communication with parents, we have successfully shifted perceptions and garnered staff buy-in to the idea that a knowledge-rich curriculum can foster both academic and personal growth.

The induction process for new teachers at Maplewell is carefully structured to ensure a smooth transition and alignment with the school's curriculum vision, as some new teachers may initially place greater emphasis on engagement over challenge, thereby sometimes undervaluing the role of a knowledge-rich curriculum for SEND students. This reflects a broader trend in many SEND schools, where success is often measured by focusing on mastering EHCP outcomes, such as developing independence, improving communication skills and managing sensory needs. While we recognise that this is both necessary and valuable, it should not become a limitation.

We also introduce our knowledge-rich curriculum to parents early, during induction and transition meetings, to build understanding and trust. While we occasionally face concerns or resistance, we remain committed to our values and clearly explain the long-term benefits for students. For those with specific needs, we make appropriate adjustments, working closely with families to ensure they feel part of the journey. Regular communication – through parents' evenings, newsletters and curriculum overviews – helps reinforce our approach. Over time, we find that parents recognise the clarity, consistency and ambition this curriculum brings, and the positive impact it has on their children's learning.

In contrast to initial parental or staff concerns, we have not faced resistance from students. Thanks to the gradual and well-sequenced build-up of knowledge and the deeply embedded pedagogical approaches we take, our students have responded with increased confidence and ambition. Over time, their self-esteem and resilience as learners have grown. Many now see opportunities that once seemed unattainable. For instance, 10 students in our current year 11 cohort have applied to study A levels at college – a next step that, at one time, would have seemed unimaginable to them, and perhaps even to us. By establishing a strong foundation but without imposing a ceiling, we enable students to reach their full potential, including achieving GCSE grades or nationally recognised qualifications.

Critics of the knowledge-rich curriculum approach sometimes argue that SEND students should prioritise life skills and core maths and English rather than engaging in academically rigorous content. While we acknowledge that a life-skills-based curriculum is essential for some students, all our curriculum pathways at Maplewell embed a knowledge-rich approach. Our experience across both mainstream and SEND settings has shown that many SEND students, in a range of educational environments, are capable of much more than is often assumed, and they should not be limited by low expectations.

Nonetheless, it is important to acknowledge the obstacles of implementing a knowledge-rich curriculum in a special needs setting, and the adaptations required. Students with retention, communication and interaction difficulties may struggle to retain and apply information effectively, which can make accessing a knowledge-rich curriculum more difficult. Traditional teaching methods may not always be suitable for students with communication difficulties, requiring educators to adapt their approaches. Additionally, teachers must carefully individualise their instruction to meet the diverse needs of their students, which demands both significant planning and flexibility. There is also a high level of need for additional support, from specialist staff and assistive technologies, which places further organisational and financial strain on the school.

Adaptations for SEND students

The implementation of the knowledge-rich curriculum at Maplewell has involved a variety of practical adaptations, particularly to meet the diverse needs of SEND students. One key aspect of this adaptation is the integration of retrieval practice – a method by which students regularly revisit previously learned material to reinforce their knowledge. This practice is especially valuable for SEND students, who may need additional repetitions to fully retain key concepts. The structured use of 'I do, we do, you do' instructional strategies also helps to support SEND students at every stage of their learning. Within this model, teachers first demonstrate the concept ('I do'), then guide students through it collaboratively ('we do'), and finally encourage students to apply it independently ('you do'). This approach allows SEND students to gradually build confidence in their understanding. Furthermore, ongoing assessments are used throughout the curriculum to check students' understanding, address knowledge gaps early and ensure continuous progress.

Adaptation plays a vital role in making the curriculum accessible to those with cognition and learning needs. For example, in a year 9 history lesson on the First World War, our teachers employ a range of strategies to support SEND learners. For a student with cognition and learning needs, the teacher might 'scaffold' with visual aids such as cause-and-effect charts to simplify complex concepts like alliances, militarism, nationalism and imperialism. By breaking down the lesson into smaller chunks, teachers provide a scaffolded learning experience. Using the 'I do, we do, you do' approach, the teacher first models the process of making connections between events, then guides students through it collaboratively, and then finally encourages independent practice. This structured approach, combined with peer support and visual tools such as timelines or video clips, helps students engage meaningfully with the content.

These adaptive strategies ensure that SEND students not only access the curriculum but also retain key knowledge, making learning both accessible and engaging. Our teachers are trained to employ such adaptive teaching techniques, including fostering fluency in essential skills and nurturing metacognitive strategies that encourage students to reflect on their learning processes and develop independence in their thinking. For example, students are regularly guided to use self-questioning techniques – such as 'What do I already know about this?' or 'What strategy worked for me last time?' – to plan, monitor and evaluate their own learning. This supports them to become more active, self-aware learners.

A knowledge-rich curriculum: Essential for SEND students

Ultimately, by maintaining a strong focus on progress monitoring, cultural capital and targeted interventions, we believe that Maplewell has been able to show that a knowledge-rich curriculum is not only achievable but *essential* for students with SEND. A knowledge-rich approach ensures that our students access the same opportunities as their mainstream peers, preparing them for a bright and successful future.

Intellectual discipline: A knowledge-rich behaviour curriculum

Tom Bennett

Recent years have seen a much-needed focus on knowledge: how this knowledge is sequenced (curriculum), how it is taught (pedagogy), and the importance of knowledge as a foundational component – if not the foundation itself – of all subsequent thinking skills, such as creativity or critical thinking. This has slowly become a norm in many educational settings. Knowledge matters – not because it is merely useful, but because it is essential.

But there is an area of education where a discussion of knowledge has been almost entirely absent, and it may be the area where it is needed most in education, even more than in the practice of teaching and learning: behaviour. At first that may not seem surprising: what has classroom or school behaviour to do with the knowledge debate, except perhaps tangentially? Normally we assume that both declarative knowledge (knowing that something is true, e.g. 'water boils at 100 degrees Celsius at sea level') and procedural knowledge (knowing how to do something, e.g. being able to replace a car tyre) are primarily concerned with success in academic fields like mathematics or practical subjects like woodwork or athletics (and of course there is considerable overlap between these two categories of knowledge).

But from my work in over 1,300 schools, I posit that *knowing-that* and *knowing-how* are also the invisible foundational components of perhaps the most important feature of a classroom: how students behave.

Behaviour is the conscious response of an organism to a stimulus from its environment. Behaviour is therefore *everything* we consciously do or say. It is the sum total of our physical actions as we interact with the world. And from that simple definition follows an equally simple but overlooked axiom of classroom practice: how the student behaves has a profound impact on the success of everything we are trying to achieve in the classroom. If a student turns up (or not) or listens (or not) or tries their best (or not) or acts civilly to their peers (or not), and a million other choices of conduct – that forms the basis of whether a student will do well at any part of their education, or the entirety of it. You could have the best curriculum and pedagogy in the world, but if the students don't listen, try hard and think about the material, or if they are too distracted or terrorised to do so, none of that will matter.

If a student doesn't 'behave', they tend not to flourish. And equally bad or worse is that others around them don't flourish either. Poor behaviour both characterises and contributes to chaos, and no child flourishes in chaos. Success in any endeavour requires focus, effort, dedication, sustained attention. This is what behaviour means – and behaviour *matters* like no other component of schooling does.

And where do our behaviours come from? Where are they learned? From our immediate surroundings, our families, our peers, our neighbourhoods, and every experience as we grow up. Consciously or not, we start to develop habits of conduct (everything from accent, to gait, to manners, to social skills, to the expectations of how to walk across a room or use cutlery) and the values that tell us, quietly and secretly, that 'These behaviours are good'.

Behaviour is knowledge is power

So, our behaviours are learned. I call this the behaviour curriculum, because it is a curriculum. It is a sequence of actions, habits and routines that comprise the total of what we do. Take a small part of this: dining etiquette. I was raised in Scotland, so by default I was shown, and observed, my family using knives and forks; I learned that one went in my left hand, and one went in my right hand. One was to cut and one was to shovel, and they could be used simultaneously for greater effect. Later, I saw my school friends from other cultures using their hands or bread to carry food to their mouths, so I tried that at their houses. At university I struggled with chopsticks in noodle bars; in formal dining I learned that the fork wasn't a shovel, but a spear; in the Middle East I tried to form balls of food in my right palm while sitting on the floor, and so on. How we eat is learned behaviour. It is performed so often that it goes from the working memory to the long-term memory, and we do it instinctively, subconsciously. Nevertheless, learned it must be. No child is born knowing how to use a knife and fork; it is 'knowledge' when we know that a knife cuts, and it is knowledge when we know how to use one. Fortunate children acquire behavioural knowledge when they are raised in circumstances that immerse them in this knowledge, through role models, explicit instruction, consistent expectations, boundaries and consequences.

In every job there are appropriate behaviours that lead to success in the role: a bus driver's ability to handle a busy road; a surgeon's skills with a scalpel, and so on. And similarly, at every moment in a school there are behaviours that lead towards or away from success in that environment. Seen in this light, good behaviour isn't just a moral question, it's a practical one. Do you *know* how to behave? Do you have the habits of behaviour that lead to habitually doing that which makes you successful? In a school, that might mean behaviours as mundane as knowing what to do in group work; knowing how to conduct oneself in assemblies; knowing how to get to the next lesson quickly; and so on. These atoms of behaviour are as ordinary as you can imagine, but they become molecules, they become substantial. With this powerful knowledge, children can be successful at school. Being without it makes all the difference.

People need to have the procedural knowledge to be able to do the right thing at the right time. Then, crucially, this has to habituated, internalised and made routine so that the correct behaviour is performed at the right time with little effort of recall. Like an experienced driver instantly knowing what to do when a car goes into a skid. This requires deliberate, repetitive, high-quality practice over and over again (another useful parallel with the academic learning process, demonstrating that learning is, indeed, learning, in whatever field).

So, what type of knowledge?

Behaviour knowledge can be sorted into three broad categories:

- *Procedural knowledge:* This is the sum total of knowledge that is required to navigate a complex environment: an airport, a public toilet, a bathroom, a ticket office, including knowing where to go, what to say and what to do. This kind of knowledge feels obvious and easy until you encounter a situation where you have no experience, like a Westerner perplexed by the operations of a Japanese electronic toilet, or a Martian walking into a barn dance. You do not know what you do not know.

- *Social knowledge:* This is the knowledge of how to behave with other people. None of this is instinctive. No one is born 'good with people'. Understanding social cues, reading others' responses, interpreting irony, picking up on hostile cues, are all part of a profoundly complex and empirical journey of discovery. This type of knowledge is vital to successfully navigating a human world.
- *Knowledge of rules and consequences:* This is knowing what is expected of us. What are the rules? What happens if I break them? What happens if I keep to them? Why are they in place?

How should schools teach this knowledge – and what knowledge should they teach?

Once we understand that behaviour is a knowledge-centred curriculum, then things get a little simpler. People tend to think behaviour is something that you are either good at or not, or that it's an entirely moral choice to do the right thing or not. But if we understand that 'the right thing' is not just a moral question but a practical one too, then it is easier to grasp that behaviour is a curriculum of practiced knowledge, procedures and techniques (leading to skills) as much as geography or acrobatics. It then follows that the way to promote good behaviour in school is therefore to teach it. And as we know a lot these days about teaching, we can apply those processes to behaviour. We have a core agreed curriculum of content. We teach students the declarative and procedural content they need, using direct instruction, then formative assessment, leaning heavily into practice to create habits, all the while relying on retrieval practice. In other words, we should teach behaviour like anything else, but with greater urgency, because success in this field contributes to success in all others. It is a profound and happy coincidence that just as education is reinvigorating itself with a renewed focus on evidence-informed practice, so too does that lens swivel around to the factor that dominates all others: student conduct, the furnace from which all other capacities are forged.

The impact of being behaviourally knowledge rich

There is an obvious theory of change implicit here: people who are taught to do something tend to perform better at it than those who are not. People who have been taught to drive are better at driving than those who have not. Teaching people to drive is not enough to guarantee good driving, or to ensure that drivers will always make good choices, but it is unquestionable that teaching the cohort in the first place is infinitely preferable to not doing so. The explanatory mechanism for knowledge-rich approaches to behaviour are axiomatically self-evident. But if the impact of being behaviourally knowledge rich were not demonstrated 'in the wild', then there would be no point. So, have we seen success in this area? Yes we have. Increasingly, and especially in England where this idea has taken root more firmly than anywhere else in the Western world, we see a burgeoning and inspirational movement in the many schools that recognise and adopt behaviour as a curriculum and have seen extraordinary dividends in terms of conduct and learning gains. Exemplar schools, from the celebrated Michaela Community School, Mercia Academy, King Solomon Academy, Charles Dickens Primary School and Bedford Free School, to the Harris Federation academies and Stanley Road Primary School, and many more, have made the deliberate choice to 'scaffold' the behavioural knowledge that children require to not merely survive but to thrive in the complex environment of institutional education.

Many of the schools listed above have frighteningly good outcomes, and this is particularly significant in light of the challenges and risk factors faced by the student cohorts they serve. It is one thing to demonstrate success in a privileged environment composed of well-supported and socially or intellectually nurtured groups of children; to see it in groups of children disproportionally exposed to disadvantage, poverty and disruption is remarkable. It is a testimony to not only the schools' ambition, but also to the strategy of taught behaviour.

As the behaviour advisor to the Department for Education (DfE) since 2015, I have been proud to be part of an institutional, national and political reform process in the English education system that has seen these ideas become normalised. The DfE's 2024 *Behaviour in Schools* guidance,[1] which I helped to write, centres the idea of the behaviour knowledge curriculum, and schools are encouraged – not mandated – to do so. This has made it possible for ambitious and capable teams to act decisively by implementing clear, assertive and structured approaches to their in-school behaviour practice, knowing that it is supported by national guidelines. Ofsted, the school inspectorate that holds so much sway in the English school system, has also advocated strongly for clear school behaviour policies that are implemented systematically, and taught diligently. Since 2024 it has aligned its inspection criteria with the DfE's behaviour guidance, resulting in a coherence of approach that was previously absent. With this unity of purpose, many schools have improved handsomely.

Pushback

With so much evidence informing this process, as well as proof of concept within the school sector, why hasn't this approach been universally embraced? The reality is that there is still a lot of pushback, resentment and disagreement with the knowledge-rich behaviour curriculum.

But the facts and the circumstances remain. Knowledge-rich perspectives on education, and the behaviour associated with that education, have been, and are, profoundly successful. How do we know that 'progressivism' doesn't lead to similar success? Before I address this, let me first briefly outline what I mean by progressivism: it is characterised by child-led education in which children are natural learners, their interests should be the guide to their curriculum, and they should be allowed as much autonomy as possible. Crucially, within this approach strict discipline is not only unnecessary, but considered actively harmful.

So, to return to the question of why it can be said that progressivism doesn't lead to the same success as a knowledge-rich approach in this context. In my view, this is for the following reasons.

1. *Lack of counter examples:* There are simply no examples of schools with challenging cohorts that succeed with minimal guidance in behaviour; without clear, well-taught boundaries and expectations; and without well-rehearsed routines and social norms. Children do not simply self-organise, no matter how much you love them, or how much independence you give them.

2. *A chaotic theory of change:* Progressivism sprung from 19th century empirical science. Given the new success of the scientific method, it was hoped that the social sciences could be equally transformed by this process,

hence 'progressivism'. But like many first drafts of social science, such as Freud's theories in psychology, what we know now has massively outstripped what they thought they knew then. The philosophy of the 19th century cannot compete with the data of the 21st century.

3. *Evidence of failure:* We find many, many examples of schools that descend into chaos when they attempt to avoid the need to teach behaviour. Whenever we see a school close through chaos, or the news reporting a near riot, or students or staff protesting because of chronic misbehaviour, there is always a backstory of permissiveness, and an over-optimistic view of human nature or the nature of society.

Without knowledge of how to behave, every other endeavour in education is obliterated. And this applies to society at any level, including, or even especially, at the classroom level, which is almost entirely composed of children who, by definition, are learning how to behave. Our approach to behaviour must also be knowledge rich. And thankfully, across the world, many are waking up to this. It is now *known*.

The role of knowledge in the school curriculum: A US case study

David Steiner

In 1988, two researchers – Donna Recht and Lauren Leslie – published what became a famous study about a group of junior high school readers who were asked to read a story about a baseball game.[1] Some of the students had been previously classified as poor readers, others as strong. Some knew about the game of baseball, others did not. What the study showed was that prior knowledge of baseball was far more important than reading skills when it came to students' ability to understand the passage.

What's surprising about the study is that anyone was surprised. The conclusion is clear: your ability to comprehend a given text depends heavily on your content knowledge of the topic of that text.

National education policies in multiple countries support this intuitively obvious finding. When countries institute a knowledge-rich curriculum and test students on learning that curriculum, students' learning grows far more than when a country either abandons, or fails to institute, such policies. As E. D. Hirsch points out in his book *Why Knowledge Matters*, in 1989 France abandoned its knowledge-rich national curriculum in favour of enabling every teacher to choose their own curricula.[2] The result was that, over the subsequent decades, every demographic of French student did worse in reading, with the most disadvantaged students suffering by far the most.[3] When countries reverse these failing policies and institute a rigorous content-rich curriculum (curricula that explicitly lay out the information students are expected to master) with integrated assessments, as England did in 2014, results have been found to rise.[4]

A specific knowledge-rich curriculum taught across a nation – or at least a province or state – is even more critical in an age of mass mobility. Imagine a child who must change schools in a given academic year, within the same city, and you are imagining the life of one-third of New York City children. Now imagine that the same child gets a different curriculum each time they move schools – they may be taught the same thing repeatedly, miss out on crucial knowledge and skills, and/or be taught subjects like mathematics in entirely different ways. Once again, it is unsurprising that American researchers find that students who are taught in public school districts that, by contrast, insist on a universally shared curriculum outperform those that allow teachers to do their own thing.[5]

In the United States, the use of a common curriculum in the 19th century (namely the McGuffey Readers)[6] fell away, due in part to the country's highly heterogeneous population; in part to a tradition of progressive education that focused on learning through experience rather than traditional teaching; and finally, in part due to a shift in educational focus from what was known as the 'melting pot' to the 'salad bowl' (creating a common identity was replaced by nurturing a diversity of identities). Instead, thousands of public school districts (of which there are approximately 12,600 across the country)[7] increasingly enabled individual teachers to act as curriculum designers, curating playlists of materials that were unique to that teacher.

The results of this shift have been deeply damaging – most especially to underprivileged children, often children of colour. The first consequence is that America's teacher preparation programmes cannot prepare teachers to teach a particular curriculum – a specific body of knowledge. Instead, these programmes prepare teachers with generic approaches that stress process (principles of how to design lessons) – approaches that are content agnostic. Second, neither the US nor individual states can assess students on any particular knowledge because students have studied such divergent material. Thus, America's typical English Language Arts (ELA) assessments – standardised tests administered by each state at the end of the academic year to evaluate reading, writing, speaking and listening – give students bits of text drawn from disparate sources and ask a series of 'skill-based' questions, such as requiring students to 'find the main idea' in a piece of writing they haven't seen before. What we find (unsurprisingly, once again) is that poor children do worse on such tests because they are less likely to have the requisite background knowledge on which comprehension depends. In response to poor results, teachers drill those students on those skills – only ensuring that they will do worse year after year, as they fall further behind their wealthier peers in terms of knowledge acquisition.

A major report published in 2018 – *The Opportunity Myth* – documented two further damaging practices that had become entrenched.[8] First, the poorer the student, the less likely she or he is to be taught rigorous materials. Second, some 80 per cent of the materials that teachers take from the internet (and over 90 per cent of America's public school teachers use such materials every week) is less academically demanding than what is expected by states for a given grade.[9] Combined with the fact that underprivileged students are disproportionately taught by first-year and/ or uncertified teachers,[10] these practices have produced widely different learning trajectories for America's school students. The National Assessment of Educational Progress

(NAEP) is the only American nationwide test in reading and mathematics, and is taken by a representative sample of 9-, 13- and 17-year-old students drawn from every state and from large cities. Results have shown sharply increasing gaps[11] – gaps that were already very large – between poor and wealthy children.

In 2011, while serving as commissioner of education for New York state, this author included a funding request to support high-quality curriculum in the state's $700 million grant application for the federal Race to the Top opportunity (a nationwide contest run by the US Department of Education that required states to establish new academic standards). The state's success in securing those funds led to our creation of the first online high-quality instructional materials (HQIM) in English Language Arts (ELA) and mathematics – materials known collectively as *EngageNY*. Made available as free, open-source materials, *EngageNY* had been downloaded across the country over 100 million times within 4 years of the release date.[12]

In Race to the Top's early years (roughly 2012–2015), HQIM simply meant curricula that were designed to meet the Common Core State Standards (CCSS) in ELA and mathematics. These standards – which laid out the skills, by year of schooling – that students were expected to master, were adopted by the great majority of America's 50 states. In the last decade, HQIM in ELA increasingly shifted from offering decontextualised drills on spelling and vocabulary combined with comprehension exercises on short bits of text, to a focus on enabling students to grapple in depth with outstanding novels, plays and short stories. Practising syntax and vocabulary is a seamless part of this intensive reading. In mathematics, once again, a laundry list of endless mathematical operations has been replaced by introducing mathematical concepts and putting practice of mathematical operations within challenging scenarios that ask students to translate narrative problems into mathematical terms.

While the sheer volume of use of *EngageNY* showed that individual teachers had an appetite for good instructional materials, it was John White, Louisiana's state superintendent (their equivalent to a state commissioner), who first championed a state-wide shift to the use of HQIM, starting in 2012. Under his leadership, the state of Louisiana adopted *Eureka Math* and then commissioned the creation of an ELA curriculum – *Guidebooks*. In addition, for its elementary school children, the state recommended a curriculum developed by the Core Knowledge Foundation – a knowledge-rich, carefully sequenced ELA programme that had been included in *EngageNY*.

In the 2024 NAEP results,[13] children in Louisiana – one of the poorest states in the US – matched the average reading performance in the country as a whole. Equally impressively, the state's fourth-grade (9-year-old) students' results showed a steady improvement that started in 2010 and continued despite the damage that the COVID-19 pandemic brought to children's learning. A second state – Mississippi – that engaged in a state-wide effort to introduce new reading curricula, and train teachers in using them, also showed continued, impressive progress in students' reading levels.

Unfortunately, the same cannot be said for some other states that had also shown some signs of improvement after being early adopters of HQIM, such as Tennessee. And the results nationwide in mathematics – even in states that have made headway in the percentage of schools using HQIM – were dismal. This wasn't a surprise: in a major 2019 study of what happens to students' achievement in mathematics after a school district adopts a new mathematics curriculum,

Harvard University researcher Thomas Kane and his colleagues found no positive impact.[14] Digging into the data, they discovered that, on average, teachers were given just over 1 day of coaching on the new materials, and that (unsurprisingly) only a quarter of the teachers subsequently used those materials for more than cursory instructional purposes.

The disappointing results in the Harvard study recall a Guinness beer advertisement from my childhood: 'I've never tried it because I don't like it.' Our research at Johns Hopkins University finds that many teachers don't believe their students can manage the rigour of the new HQIM, and thus don't use the materials, or that they water them down to the point where they lose their efficacy altogether.[15]

To address this situation, attention in the US has shifted from persuading school districts to adopt HQIM, to assisting districts and their schools to enable teachers to overcome their resistance to HQIM and thus to implement these materials in their classrooms. Clearly, coaching teachers more extensively is part of the answer. But there is a deeper problem: HQIM are designed to be rigorous grade-level curricula, and America's teachers aren't wrong in believing that most of their students aren't ready for the academic demands embedded in these materials. The majority of students in both mathematics and ELA perform below the proficiency standard on the NAEP.

If we are going to shift teachers' views on HQIM, school districts will need to think hard about providing extra support and time for students who would otherwise be unable to successfully access HQIM classes. This extra time (usually 45–90 minutes a week) is often labelled 'Tier 2 instruction'. This is to distinguish it from Tier 1 instruction, which is the regular class time devoted to teaching the HQIM curriculum. To date, however, the way Tier 2 instruction is given – and which students are given that extra instruction – has been a largely unregulated and messy domain of instruction, often unrelated to Tier 1 materials.

What is needed are good diagnostic assessments linked to each specific HQIM curriculum that tell teachers which students need what kind of support at what point in the semester (the school term).[16] The idea is that at the start of the year, students would take a test that would assess the degree to which they were ready to learn the HQIM for that academic year. Teachers would get an assessment report that would identify which students showed a lack of the necessary prerequisite knowledge and skills, and when during the year those skills would be needed. That way, Tier 2 instructional time could be properly aligned to which students needed what academic support and when they needed it. We are beginning to see education technology companies such as ANet[17] and Modern Classrooms[18] offering early versions of such diagnostic software.

Two things are clear from both research and school district-level results. When implemented effectively (in states such as Louisiana and in school districts such as Houston, Texas), HQIM can make a real difference to student results. Effective implementation, as described above, includes diagnostic assessments, effective planning for Tier 2 instruction, professional development for teachers to ensure that they are deeply familiar with the HQIM they are expected to teach, and a commitment from their school principals and school district leadership to support effective implementation. In the case of principals, this means that their classroom observations should include checking that teachers are using their HQIM as intended (or can explain any departures from doing so). As for school district leaders, they need to support the necessary professional development for teachers.

Such full, integrated HQIM implementation is still quite rare: the norm is that teachers in the US are (understandably) reluctant to use instructional materials that presuppose a level of learning that the majority of students lack. The solutions discussed above may help ameliorate the challenges, but these solutions will work best with students who are only modestly behind. With students whose learning is several years in arrears, the solutions lie elsewhere – with a wholesale rethinking of pre-Kindergarten education and the economic and social policies that create massive disparities in readiness to learn among America's children. Specifically, attention has to be paid to the pre-Kindergarten years, where the inequalities of learning outcomes are already established and then prove so difficult to overcome.

From the earliest reading instruction, offering all students – especially those who are underprivileged – access to the building blocks of knowledge is essential to their long-term educational success.

The fragility of knowledge in England's schools

Christine Counsell

Those of us persuaded by the power of knowledge in education have good reason to fear its demise. Whenever any valuable cultural shift is taken for granted, its fall is likely. Such falls are normally from grace of tradition to bane of routine, but in the case of England's knowledge revolution in schools, much work remains to establish the tradition itself.

This essay argues that lack of policy attention to professional understanding of knowledge itself, particularly in senior educational leadership, renders the knowledge revolution dangerously fragile.

Five springs of the knowledge revolution

The turn to knowledge in England has various, philosophically distinct origins. At least five disparate wellsprings have fed it.

First is the role of wide knowledge in improving literacy among the disadvantaged. Popularised by E. D. Hirsch, this argument fused cultural and psychological premises. E. D. Hirsch explained how background knowledge transforms the speed of meaning-making that enables fluent reading.[1] A student's vocabulary size is the outward result of an inward acquisition of knowledge. Texts therefore depend on reader and writer sharing common knowledge.[2]

The second is a very different disciplinary spring, albeit driven by similar passion for equity. Associated with sociologist Michael Young and emerging from an international social realist movement, it concerns the inherent powers of 'specialised' or academic knowledge as opposed to 'everyday' knowledge.[3] That such knowledge is produced by disciplinary experts gives it two qualities. First, because it is systematic, it produces abstract concepts. These transform possibilities for human thought, interaction and creativity. Second, because it is constantly renewed by those disciplines, this knowledge is provisional and revisable. School subjects, argues Michael Young, as vehicles for teaching disciplinary traditions, are therefore emancipatory. Far from preserving elites, they distribute power, and should be taught to all young people, regardless of future employment.[4]

The third wellspring, often forgotten, is active communities of subject teachers.[5] Through the decades in which generic or cross-curricular skills were promoted in leadership training, some subject teachers lived professional lives of resistance. They analysed and debated the teaching of knowledge through their own curricular theorising.[6] History, in particular, having had a skills revolution earlier than most, had its own, early knowledge comeback.[7] The integration of substantive knowledge into a disciplinary approach has long been theorised in sophisticated ways by history teachers themselves.[8]

Fourth is a shift in educational assessment whose significance for England's 'knowledge turn' has been profound. New assessment theory has exposed two closely related flaws in assessment practice: a misuse of summative assessments and a mistaken adoption of skill-based level descriptors (such as examination mark schemes or generic levels) as progression models.[9] The mistake in each case is to treat practising the final performance – say, GCSE examination or year 6 SATs test – as the means and measure of progress. Any journey towards success requires many components which may not resemble the final performance but which are, in fact, the best guides of progress towards it. In other words, formative assessment should be decoupled from summative. We should assess whatever components cumulatively assure progress.[10]

When the chasing of surface performance is exposed as less effective than mastering hidden components, the function of knowledge is revealed. A good example is that of fluent reading, mentioned above. Research shows that practising 'skills' of inference (typical of England's year 6 SATs test and a perfectly effective *summative* test of reading capability) has limited impact.[11] Wide knowledge from a broad curriculum, however, through its impact on students' vocabulary and idiom, has substantial and durable effect. It is prior knowledge that makes new material accessible; for schema stored in long-term memory change what our brains 'see' or recognise.[12]

What matters therefore, in ongoing or formative assessment, is regular checking of curriculum mastery, not the repeated, premature replication of a final summative test. As educator and writer Michael Fordham famously expressed, the curriculum *is* the progression model.[13] This changes what a teacher looks for both in planning and in assessment: you become interested in what the knowledge is *doing* and whether it is secure.

My fifth and final wellspring is the one best known: the application of the cognitive science of memory to learning. This vital research domain, first popularised by teacher-led grassroots movements, is now enshrined in England's formal suite of professional qualifications, from the Initial Teacher Training and Early Career Framework (ITTECF) to leadership national professional qualifications (NPQs).[14]

Cognitive science is the wellspring most commonly associated with knowledge and is sometimes treated as synonymous with it. It is also the one that says least about knowledge itself. Influential gurus of evidence-led pedagogy, such as Barak Rosenshine, powerfully explain underlying cognitive mechanisms that make learning happen, but say much less about the vital professional work of choosing, configuring, shaping and texturing the thing to be learned.[15] You cannot Rosenshine your way into a curriculum, and nor can you Rosenshine your way into mediating content in subject-sensitive ways.

And so we have a strange state of affairs. England's national professional qualifications rightly emphasise how knowledge supports understanding, how to ensure students remember it, how to chunk and pace content, but not how knowledge's distinctive disciplinary presentations affect such mediation. Qualification frameworks shout knowledge, but by rendering principles for teaching generic, they conceal the object to be learned – knowledge itself. Guidance on what to do with content – whether to chunk, pace, space, explain or retrieve it – is ubiquitous, but generic.

Knowledge and curriculum

England's most far-reaching shift towards knowledge came not through national professional qualifications, nor through a revised national curriculum, but with Ofsted's unprecedented attention to curriculum in 2019.[16]

The shift was far-reaching chiefly because accountability is a powerful lever, but also because it drew on all five of the above springs. By incentivising schools to switch from being assessment-led to being curriculum-led, the 2019 education inspection framework (EIF) placed knowledge at the heart of its theory of change.[17] Ofsted's espousal of knowledge challenged short-termist notions of school improvement. If a school is improving results chiefly by throwing the kitchen sink at year 6 or 11, then the school will still be doing that in 10 years' time. For *the school* to truly improve, it must transform the student long before they reach the test. That is what curriculum is for: it is there to change the child. Broad, secure knowledge changes what students perceive, recognise and can do, freeing up memory space and driving curiosity for the new.

Led by the then chief inspector Amanda Spielman, Ofsted performed a *volte face* in three ways.

- It became critical of reliance on summative assessments (e.g. GCSE questions) as ways of planning for or measuring progress. The burden of proof for securing progress was to lie in curriculum quality.
- This new interest in the quality of input meant an interest in knowledge itself and, therefore, subjects.
- It no longer judged teaching separately from its curricular object – the thing being learned.

Developments dependent on compliance rather than conviction, however, are fragile.[18] And such drinking from all five springs of the knowledge revolution is far from embedded across the sector. I will now examine two manifestations of this fragility and consider what each might reveal about missing layers in leaders' understanding of knowledge.

Signs of fragility 1: Resistance to knowledge
Many educationists remain unclear about the functions of knowledge in raising achievement. Two misconceptions are common.

First, a belief in the false god of the exam-derived skill hierarchy as means and measure of progress stubbornly persists. In some formative assessment practice, this unreliable measure of progress continues to supplant assessment of curriculum mastery. An Ofsted subject review in 2023 reported that, despite clear discouragement from the EIF, around 50 per cent of history departments still used GCSE-style questions in key stage 3 in mistaken belief that early rehearsal of these examination-derived skills would develop and demonstrate progress.[19]

Likewise in primary reading, leading experts in evidence-informed practice report that they *still* need to bang the drum that the ability to make inferences at speed comes from wide background knowledge, and that constant rehearsal of the fiddly comprehension questions in SATs reading tests, quite apart from being soul-crushingly dull, is very limited in efficacy.[20]

What is going wrong here? Why do leaders cling to discredited practices in place of long-term attention to curriculum substance?

The answer may be simple – that the false logic of treating skill hierarchies as progression models is highly seductive. Their repeated recurrence over the past 35 years would suggest this.[21] But any propensity for leaders to be seduced must betray limited awareness of the effects of knowledge – its effects on vocabulary size, agile thinking, speedy comprehension and much else besides that drives long-term transformation towards examination success.

A second, entirely different, resistance to knowledge is an assumption that it leads to dreary, joyless learning dominated by dry rehearsal of facts. This misconception, too, turns out to be rooted in a weak professional grasp of knowledge, but this time of its nature. For knowledge is not information. It is not comprised of lists of facts, but of connections and relationships held together by structures, textures and flows.

These structures, textures and flows create different types of account, many of which require artistry in order to be meaningful or to be apprehended at all. Think storytelling in history, the textures of literature, argument in many subjects, music itself. If mere information were being taught, rather than these distinctive accounts, dryness would indeed result, and as we'll see in our final section, arguably *knowledge* would not be being taught at all.

Signs of fragility 2: 'Knowledge-rich gone wrong'
Perhaps the most serious misunderstanding of knowledge is one hiding in plain sight. This arises not among those reluctant to trust it, but in schools which sincerely believe that they support it. In such settings, it is now common to see required lesson structures which cause profound difficulties in subjects for which they are unsuited. Such structures are informed by cognitive science of learning, but not by consideration of knowledge itself.[22]

Figure 1: Curricular object treated as procedure

In these approaches, the main objects of learning are construed as **procedures**.	
Example 1 **All lessons must be structured using these stages:**	Example 2 **All lessons must be structured using these stages:**
Retrieve	Connect
Explain	Explain
Model	Practice
Assess	Consolidate
Deliberate practice	Oral practice (vocabulary work)
Evaluate	Retrieve and apply

Note: The archetypes shown here are composites which the author has created from a range of whole-school or programme practices of this type.

Figure 2: Curricular object treated as proposition

In this approach, the main objects of learning are construed as **propositions**.

All lessons in our school must begin with an explicit statement of:
• the vocabulary to be learned
• three or four facts or propositions that the lesson will teach.

Students must be able to say or write the following at the starts/ends of lessons:
• In this lesson I will learn these four things: ...
• In this lesson I have learned these four things: ...

The examples in Figures 1 and 2 reduce knowledge to propositions or procedures. Yet much of the time in the humanities, arts and literature, one is not teaching a procedure, nor anything reducible to propositions. Evidence-informed practices such as modelling, regular retrieval, reducing cognitive load or making connections are vital, but their arrangement in standard structures takes no account of subject-specific textures, forms and flows in which knowledge presents itself. Nor does it take account of the disciplinary status of each claim being taught – its provisionality or degree of certainty – and resulting distinctions of claim, argument, interpretation or fact. Without attention to these, a subject is flattened into information.

Let's consider one aspect of 'flow'. Figure 3 captures an effective approach to history lesson sequences, one well-theorised by teachers of truly knowledge-rich history.[23] Disciplinary meaning is made as two parallel journeys interact – a narrative journey and an analytic journey.

Figure 3: The dynamic driving a sequence of history lessons

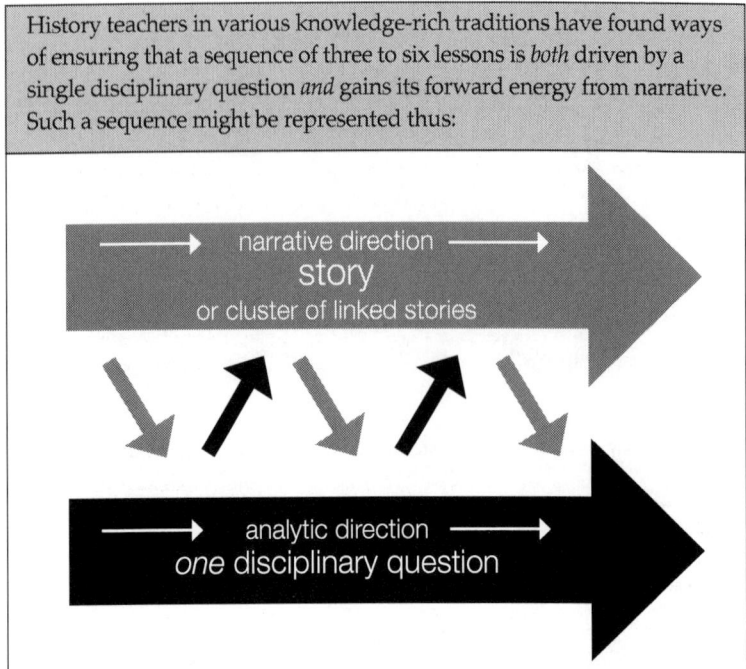

Such a knowledge-rich journey can be tightly structured, carefully paced and thoroughly taught without reducing it to practising procedures. Indeed, if each lesson *were* built around a procedure, we would lose the coherence and efficacy that derive from the sequence's culmination: the student steadily shaping an argument in response to one disciplinary question. To reduce historical reasoning and argument to procedure has long been demonstrated as poor practice.[24] Equally, to judge the success of one lesson in that journey by mastery of propositions, ignoring how content is positioned and heralded by surrounding narrative and disciplinary direction, is to fail to appreciate how the form and flow of knowledge is driving understanding.[25]

In 2016, I wrote 'Genericism's children', an exposé of the frustration and despair that knowledge-committed secondary subject leaders were experiencing in the face of whole-school practices which neglected subject rigour.[26] It is a tragic irony that 10 years on, genericism has returned, but this time in the name of knowledge.[27]

What do senior leaders need to know about knowledge?

Genericism damages knowledge because it flattens subjects into information. Knowledge comes from disciplines. Disciplinary textures, forms and flows give it meaning. If we are not attending to disciplinary features, we are not attending to knowledge. Genericism is inevitable if instead of attending to knowledge, leaders take the object of study for granted.

If policymakers are serious about the powers of knowledge for inclusion, equity and standards, then urgent attention to knowledge itself is necessary in the training of senior leaders. Unsurprisingly, where intensive attention exists, it is within well-established subject communities. But the gains of such communities are fragile, and any knowledge-rich revolution doomed if school leadership teams – those who sit above subjects – unwittingly erode them.

Currently, NPQs at senior levels – senior leadership, headship and executive level – scarcely address this.[28] School and system leaders still lack serious induction into one of the hardest leaps of all – transcending one's own subject and taking assurance from middle leaders of other subject specialisms.

So, what might education's senior leaders be studying if knowledge traditions are to be established and renewed? I suggest a five-point syllabus to start the debate.

1. Leaders must be equipped to ask questions arising from the temporal qualities of curriculum.
We cannot appraise a curriculum via audit, only as a narrative. Curriculum is knowledge structured as narrative

over time. Each lesson is oriented to the future and gathering a past.

Just as with narrative, the effects of earlier knowledge on later understanding are often highly indirect. Vocabulary rendered secure 3 years ago surfaces in students' speed, agility, creative thought or curiosity. The immediate impact of secure knowledge is observable and rapid, but its powerful relationship with eventual outcomes may be invisible. The word 'curriculum', from the Latin *currere* (to run a course), implies a journey. To be curriculum-led is to see the role of each part of the journey, rather than seeking illusionary shortcuts to the destination.

An orientation to this temporal quality of curriculum enables senior leaders to ask subject leaders questions about what particular knowledge moments or aspects are 'doing' within wider timescales.[29]

2. Leaders must examine whether students are thriving in the now.

Despite its orientation to the future, in a truly knowledge-*rich* curriculum, just as in a narrative, the in-the-moment joy or intrinsic value of the moment is, paradoxically, enhanced. We don't enjoy narratives (think novels and films) just to get to the endpoint. Rather, we relish each moment, and each moment evokes a quality of the whole. In a curriculum, likewise, the gratification is not all deferred. The gratification is also in the now, in the satisfaction of mastery or the compulsive rewards of anticipation. It also comes from being inducted into new kinds of belonging, into new identities, which distinct subject communities distinctively bestow. Gratification comes from the beauty and dignity of the curricular object. A lesson is not merely forward-projecting; its pleasure is intrinsic.

Take English literature. The experience of reading novels matters. Particular novels matter in fostering enjoyment of related ones. When an objective to recall 'character, setting, plot and theme', or to deploy a skill, becomes the point, we can lose the educative purpose of reading novels. (We also lose memorable and meaningful methods for achieving precisely those objectives!) Students cannot authentically discuss 'effect on the reader' if the text has had no effect on the reader.[30]

It is vital not to confuse this with gimmicks for 'engagement'. It is rather that a student remembering *what it meant to come to know in the first place*, is part of knowing. The text, the music, the art, the argument has an effect in the moment of encounter and that encounter matters: it becomes part of the knowledge.

This is easily lost when a generic lesson structure is imposed on subject content. The shape, pattern or texture of the knowledge flow is not driving the configuration of learning activity. Instead, what needs asking is: how should this poem, this geographical question, this historical story, this philosophical principle, this sound-world, this painting be encountered? Where does that encounter sit and fit with prior and later encounter? What mix of propositions, composite accounts (narratives, arguments, descriptions), aesthetic appreciation, open questioning and wonder is necessary for shaping that encounter?

In the dawn of an AI revolution, we must teach what it means to be human. Literary text is prized even in a utility-driven educational age because imagery sings and observations are spry and arresting. It is not that AI cannot recognise this (it can), it is what it does to us as humans to recognise it.

3. Leaders need to know about semantic gravity.

What we might call the texture of a subject is related to a discipline's semantic gravity – the extent to which it is naturally 'pulled down' (like gravity) into particulars or detail.[31] Disciplines with weak semantic gravity (such as science) can be communicated at the level of general principles, laws and regularities. Disciplines with strong semantic gravity, however, are quickly distorted and hard to assimilate if they linger too long on high-level generalisations. Students only make sense of religions, art, fiction or the crowded scenery of the past, through a hinterland of detail: stories at human scale, the froth of human drama, a steady world-building into sense of place, period or atmosphere.

A conversation between general and particular enlivens all subjects, but that conversation differs markedly across science and history, music and mathematics. Semantic gravity is a way of talking about this across subjects.

4. Leaders must learn to enquire about the status of knowledge.

This is the disciplinary dimension of the subject – what students learn about the types of question that philosophers, geographers or scientists typically ask, and about their standards of truth claims or their notions of evidence. It is where students learn about the conditions under which valid claims can be made. For each school subject refers to a discipline or practice, outside of school, that is a distinctive quest for truth.[32]

We cannot appraise a lesson's quality if we are unclear about the degree of certainty attached to a claim or what part it plays in steadily revealing a certain type of disciplinary puzzle.

5. Leaders need to understand why teachers need a relationship with the knowledge that they teach.

Knowledge is profoundly relational. Social in its origins and its renewal, to teach it well is to model being an educated adult enriched by the material and thriving on discussing it with others, in community – whether in cultural practices of making art and music, in lifelong habits of reading and discussing novels, in staying engaged with the sources and purposes of new scholarship and science. Engagement with teacher subject communities is also essential for renewal of the curricular expression of all this.[33]

Conclusion

I want to conclude by suggesting three reasons why these issues are of critical importance, right now. The first two are currently much discussed:

- a crisis of engagement in students;
- a crisis of recruitment and retention in teachers.

The third is rarely discussed:

- a crisis in standards.

'Standards' has come to mean '*measure of* standards' but it ought also to mean intrinsic quality – the rigour and value of what and how we teach. A question that needs sustained debate in policy and leadership circles is what the school experience of history, chemistry, literature or art is worth. Is it providing an authentic and lasting introduction to these domains? Or has it been supplanted by proxies and formulae that have lost their way?

Endnotes

Defining a knowledge-rich curriculum, *Ruth Ashbee*

1   Faloyin, D. (2022) *Africa Is Not A Country*. London: Harvill Secker.
2   Hartshorne, J. K. and Makovski, T. (2019) 'The effect of working memory maintenance on long-term memory' in *Memory and Cognition*, 2019;47(4):749–763. Available at: https://pubmed.ncbi.nlm.nih.gov/31073790/ (accessed 10/11/25).
3   Surma, T. *et al* (2025) 'Knowledge and the Curriculum' in *Developing Curriculum for Deep Thinking*. SpringerBriefs in Education. Cham, Switzerland: Springer. Available at: https://doi.org/10.1007/978-3-031-74661-1_3 (accessed 10/11/25).

Knowledge-rich curricula: A key driver of equity in education, *Dylan Wiliam*

1   Organisation for Economic Co-operation and Development (2000) *Measuring Student Knowledge and Skills: The PISA 2000 Assessment of Reading, Mathematical and Scientific Literacy*. Available at: www.oecd.org/en/publications/2000/04/measuring-student-knowledge-and-skills_g1gh267b.html (accessed 16/10/25).
2   Department for Education and Skills (2005) *Departmental Report 2005*. Available at: www.gov.uk/government/publications/department-for-education-and-skills-departmental-report-2005 (accessed 16/10/25).
3   For example, Melby-Lervåg, M. and Hulme, C. (2013) 'Is working memory training effective? A meta-analytic review' in *Developmental Psychology*, 2013;49(2):270–291. Available at: https://doi.org/10.1037/a0028228 (accessed 16/10/25).
4   Torrance, E. P. and Templeton, D. E. (1963) *Minnesota tests of creative thinking*. University of Minnesota College of Education.
5   Schneider, W. *et al* (1989) 'Domain-Specific Knowledge and Memory Performance: A Comparison of High- and Low-Aptitude Children' in *Journal of Educational Psychology*, 1989;81(3):306–312. Available at: www.researchgate.net/publication/38138539_Domain-Specific_Knowledge_and_Memory_Performance_A_Comparison_of_High-_and_Low-Aptitude_Children (accessed 16/10/25).

6   Ray, A. (2008) 'Australia brought down to earth' in *The Guardian*,
     20 January. Available at: www.theguardian.com/sport/2008/
     jan/20/cricket.sport (accessed 16/10/25).
7   Hirsch Jr., E. D. (2016) *Why Knowledge Matters: Rescuing our Children
     from Failed Educational Theories.* Cambridge, MA: Harvard Education
     Press.
8   Sultana, F. *et al* (2025) 'An Evaluation of Secondary School Students'
     Use and Understanding of Learning Strategies to Study and Revise
     for Science Examinations' in *Education Sciences*, 2025;15(1):101.
     Available at: www.mdpi.com/2227-7102/15/1/101 (accessed
     16/10/25).
9   Willingham, D. (2023) *Outsmart Your Brain: Why Learning is Hard and
     How You Can Make it Easy.* New York: Gallery Books.

**Why not everyone has been convinced about the benefits of a
knowledge-rich curriculum,** *Joshua Vallance*

1   Ofsted (2019) *Education inspection framework (EIF).* Available at:
     www.gov.uk/government/publications/education-inspection-
     framework (accessed 16/10/25).
2   Ofsted (2021) *Curriculum research reviews: Subject reports.* Available
     at: www.gov.uk/government/collections/curriculum-research-
     reviews (accessed 16/10/25).
3   Gibb, N. (2015) 'How E. D. Hirsch Came to Shape UK Government
     Policy' in Simons, J. and Porter, N. (eds) *Knowledge and the
     Curriculum.* London: Policy Exchange. Available at: https://
     policyexchange.org.uk/publication/knowledge-and-the-
     curriculum-a-collection-of-essays-to-accompany-e-d-hirschs-lecture-
     at-policy-exchange/ (accessed 16/10/25).
4   See: www.coreknowledge.org/meet-founder-e-d-hirsch-jr/
     (accessed 16/10/25).
5   Department for Education and Gibb, N. (2018) 'School Standards
     Minister at ResearchED' on Gov.uk, 8 September. Available at:
     www.gov.uk/government/speeches/school-standards-minister-at-
     researched (accessed 16/10/25).
6   Ofsted and Spielman, A. (2019) 'Amanda Spielman at the "Wonder
     Years" curriculum conference' on Gov.uk, 26 January. Available at:
     www.gov.uk/government/speeches/amanda-spielman-at-the-
     wonder-years-curriculum-conference (accessed 16/10/25).

7   Young, M. (2014) *The curriculum and the entitlement to knowledge*.
    Cambridge Assessment Network and Research. Available at: www.
    cambridgeassessment.org.uk/Images/166279-the-curriculum-and-
    the-entitlement-to-knowledge-prof-michael-young.pdf (accessed
    16/10/25).

8   Young, M. *et al* (2014) *Knowledge and the Future School: Curriculum
    and Social Justice*. London: Bloomsbury Publishing, p71.

9   Ibid, pxv.

10 Enser, M. (2024) 'Powerful knowledge: what teachers need to
    understand' in *Tes magazine*, 10 April. Available at: www.tes.com/
    magazine/teaching-learning/general/powerful-knowledge-what-
    teachers-need-to-understand (accessed 16/10/25).

11 Ford, A. (2022) 'Why is "powerful knowledge" failing to forge a
    path to the future of history education?' in *History Education Research
    Journal*, 2022;19(1)3. Available at: https://doi.org/10.14324/
    HERJ.19.1.03 (accessed 16/10/25).

12 Freire, P. (1970) *Pedagogy of the Oppressed*. New York: Seabury Press.

13 Alam, M. (2013) 'Banking Model of Education in Teacher-Centered
    Class: A Critical Assessment' in *Research on Humanities and Social
    Sciences*, 2013;3(15)27–30. Available at: https://core.ac.uk/
    reader/234673640 (accessed 16/10/25).

14 See, for example, Department for Education and Gibb, N. (2021)
    'The importance of a knowledge-rich curriculum' on Gov.uk,
    21 July. Available at: www.gov.uk/government/speeches/the-
    importance-of-a-knowledge-rich-curriculum (accessed 16/10/25).

15 Ibid.

16 Ofsted (2019) *Education inspection framework: overview of research*.
    Available at: www.gov.uk/government/publications/education-
    inspection-framework-overview-of-research (accessed 16/10/25).

17 See, for example, https://stjosephsgateshead.bwcet.com/wp-
    content/uploads/2023/11/OFSTED-report-St-Josephs-Catholic.pdf
    (accessed 16/10/25).

18 Sehgal Cuthbert, A. and Standish, A. (eds) (2021) *What Should
    Schools Teach? Disciplines, subjects and the pursuit of truth*. Second
    edition. London: UCL Press. Available at: https://uclpress.co.uk/
    book/what-should-schools-teach/ (accessed 16/10/25).

19 Byrom, J. *et al* (1997) *Medieval Minds: Britain 1066–1500 (Think
    Through History)*. London: Pearson Longman.

20 Ofsted (2021) *Research review series: history*. Available at: www.gov.
    uk/government/publications/research-review-series-history/
    research-review-series-history (accessed 16/10/25).

The limitations of knowledge: A constructive challenger perspective,
Jim Knight

1   Department for Education (2023) 'England among highest performing western countries in education' on Gov.uk, 5 December. Available at: www.gov.uk/government/news/england-among-highest-performing-western-countries-in-education (accessed 16/10/25).

2   Department for Education (2023) 'England moves to fourth in international rankings for reading' on Gov.uk, 16 May. Available at: www.gov.uk/government/news/england-moves-to-fourth-in-international-rankings-for-reading (accessed 16/10/25).

3   Bradshaw, J. *et al* (2010) *Programme for International Student Assessment 2009: achievement of 15-year-olds in England*. London: Department for Education and National Foundation for Educational Research. Available at: www.gov.uk/government/publications/programme-for-international-student-assessment-2009-achievement-of-15-year-olds-in-england (accessed 16/10/25).

4   Sizmur, J. *et al* (2019) *Achievement of 15-year-olds in England: PISA 2018 results, Research report*. London: Department for Education and National Foundation for Educational Research. Available at: www.gov.uk/government/publications/pisa-2018-national-report-for-england (accessed 16/10/25).

5   Ingram, J. *et al* (2023) *PISA 2022: National Report for England, Research report*. London: Department for Education and Oxford University. Available at: www.gov.uk/government/publications/pisa-2022-national-report-for-england (accessed 16/10/25).

6   Ibid.

7   Kuhn, L. *et al* (2021) *PISA 2018 additional analyses: What does PISA tell us about the wellbeing of 15-year-olds? Research brief*. London: Department for Education and National Foundation for Educational Research, p4. Available at: https://assets.publishing.service.gov.uk/media/6022781ce90e0711ce41370e/Wellbeing_research_brief_England.pdf (accessed 16/10/25).

8   Ingram, J. *et al* (2023) *PISA 2022: National Report for England, Research report*, pp119–120. London: Department for Education and Oxford University. Available at: www.gov.uk/government/publications/pisa-2022-national-report-for-england (accessed 16/10/25).

9   Organisation for Economic Co-operation and Development (2023) *PISA 2022 Database*, Volume II, Annex B1, Chapter 1, Table II.B1.1.10: 'Students' life satisfaction'; and Volume II, Annex B2, Table II.B2.2: 'Students' life satisfaction'. Available at: www.oecd.org/en/data/datasets/pisa-2022-database.html (accessed 16/10/25).

10 Organisation for Economic Co-operation and Development (2023) *PISA 2022 Database*, Volume II, Annex B2, Table II.B2.15: 'Long-term student absenteeism from primary to upper secondary school'. Available at: www.oecd.org/en/data/datasets/pisa-2022-database.html (accessed 16/10/25).

11 Organisation for Economic Co-operation and Development (2023) *PISA 2022 Database*, Volume II, Annex B1, Chapter 3, Table II.B1.3.49: 'Long-term student absenteeism from primary to upper secondary school'. Available at: www.oecd.org/en/data/datasets/pisa-2022-database.html (accessed 16/10/25).

12 Department for Education (2025) 'Teacher retention' in *School workforce in England*. Available at: https://explore-education-statistics.service.gov.uk/find-statistics/school-workforce-in-england#dataBlock-a47f5dc9-567f-4385-8bff-7e01e249884e-tables (accessed 16/10/25).

13 Department for Education (2025) 'Leavers' in *School workforce in England*. Available at: https://explore-education-statistics.service.gov.uk/find-statistics/school-workforce-in-england#dataBlock-a47f5dc9-567f-4385-8bff-7e01e249884e-tables (accessed 16/10/25).

14 Office for National Statistics (2025) *Young people not in education, employment or training (NEET), UK*. Available at: www.ons.gov.uk/employmentandlabourmarket/peoplenotinwork/unemployment/bulletins/youngpeoplenotineducationemploymentortrainingneet/february2025 (accessed 16/10/25).

15 Universities and Colleges Admissions Service (2025) 'UCAS releases undergraduate January equal consideration applicant data for 2025', 13 February. Available at: www.ucas.com/corporate/news-and-key-documents/news/ucas-releases-undergraduate-january-equal-consideration-applicant-data-2025 (accessed 16/10/25).

16 Department for Education (2024) *GCSE English and maths results*. Available at: www.ethnicity-facts-figures.service.gov.uk/education-skills-and-training/11-to-16-years-old/a-to-c-in-english-and-maths-gcse-attainment-for-children-aged-14-to-16-key-stage-4/latest/ (accessed 16/10/25).

17 Joint Council for Qualifications (2025) *GCSE (Full Course) Outcomes for Post-16 for England: English Language and Mathematics, Results November 2024 (England only, aged 18, figure for 2023)*, p3.

18 Times Education Commission (2022) *Bringing out the Best: How to transform education and unleash the potential of every child*. Available at: https://nuk-tnl-editorial-prod-staticassets.s3.amazonaws.com/2022/education-commission/Times%20Education%20Commission%20final%20report.pdf (accessed 16/10/25).

19 HMC (2021) *The State of Education – Time to Talk*. Available at: www.hmc.org.uk/reports/state-of-education-time-to-talk-an-hmc-report/ (accessed 16/10/25).

20 Coulter, S. *et al* (2022) *Ending the Big Squeeze on Skills: How to Futureproof Education in England*. London: Tony Blair Institute for Global Change. Available at: https://institute.global/insights/public-services/ending-big-squeeze-skills-how-futureproof-education-england (accessed 16/10/25).

21 Cambridge OCR (2024) *Striking the balance: A review of 11–16 curriculum and assessment in England*. Available at: https://teach.ocr.org.uk/striking-the-balance (accessed 16/10/25).

22 House of Lords Education for 11–16 Year Olds Committee (2023) *Requires improvement: urgent change for 11–16 education*. Available at: https://publications.parliament.uk/pa/ld5804/ldselect/ldedu1116/17/1702.htm (accessed 16/10/25).

23 House of Lords Education for 11–16 Year Olds Committee (2023) *Corrected oral evidence: Education for 11–16 year olds (Evidence Session No. 3)*, 27 April. Available at: https://committees.parliament.uk/oralevidence/13095/pdf/ (accessed 16/10/25).

24 Coulter, S. *et al* (2022) *Ending the Big Squeeze on Skills: How to Futureproof Education in England*. London: Tony Blair Institute for Global Change. Available at: https://institute.global/insights/public-services/ending-big-squeeze-skills-how-futureproof-education-england (accessed 16/10/25).

25 House of Lords Education for 11–16 Year Olds Committee (2023) *Corrected oral evidence: Education for 11–16 year olds (Evidence Session No. 14)*, 13 July. Available at: https://committees.parliament.uk/oralevidence/13538/html/ (accessed 16/10/25).

26 Ibid.

27 Campaign for the Arts (2024) 'Exam results show further collapse in arts enrolment, deepening a 15-year decline', 15 August. Available at: www.campaignforthearts.org/news/exam-results-show-further-collapse-in-arts-enrolment-deepening-a-15-year-decline/ (accessed 16/10/25).

28 Wolf, A. (2011) *Review of Vocational Education – The Wolf Report*. London: Department for Education and Department for Business, Innovation & Skills. Available at: www.gov.uk/government/publications/review-of-vocational-education-the-wolf-report (accessed 16/10/25).

29   Ofqual (2025) *Vocational and other qualifications over time.* Available at: https://analytics.ofqual.gov.uk/apps/VTQ/ VocationalAndOtherQualificationsOverTime/ (accessed 16/10/25).

30   For example, Credly. Available at: https://info.credly.com/ (accessed 16/10/25).

Knowledge and skills: A journey not a dichotomy, *Clare Sealy*

1   Chartered Institute of Personnel and Development (2022) *Employer views on skills policy in the UK.* Available at: www.cipd.org/uk/ knowledge/reports/employer-skills-view-uk/ (accessed 16/10/25).

2   Ingram, J. *et al* (2023) *PISA 2022: National Report for England, Research report.* London: Department for Education and Oxford University. Available at: www.gov.uk/government/publications/pisa-2022-national-report-for-england (accessed 16/10/25).

3   Golding, J. *et al* (2024) *Trends in International Mathematics and Science Study (TIMSS) 2023: National report for England Volume 1.* London: Department for Education. Available at: www.gov.uk/government/ publications/trends-in-international-mathematics-and-science-study-2023-england (accessed 16/10/25).

4   Roberts, N. *et al* (2024) *Educational attainment of boys.* London: House of Commons Library. Available at: https://commonslibrary. parliament.uk/research-briefings/cdp-2024-0043/ (accessed 16/10/25).

5   Willingham, D. (2009) *Why Don't Our Students Like School?*, pp21–22. San Francisco, CA: Jossey-Bass.

6   Kirschner P. *et al* (2006) 'Why Minimal Guidance During Instruction Does Not Work: An Analysis of the Failure of Constructivist, Discovery, Problem-Based, Experiential, and Inquiry-Based Teaching' in *Educational Psychologist*, 2006;41(2):75–86. Available at: www.tandfonline.com/doi/abs/10.1207/s15326985ep4102_1 (accessed 16/10/25).

7   Ofsted (2024) *School inspection handbook.* Available at: www.gov.uk/ government/publications/school-inspection-handbook-eif/school-inspection-handbook-for-september-2023 (accessed 16/10/25).

8   Hirsch Jr., E. D. (2000) '"You can always look it up" … or can you?' in *American Educator*, 2000;24(1):4–9. Available at: www.aft.org/ae/ spring2000 (accessed 16/10/25).

9   Busch, B. (ed) (2025) '5 studies that explain why students can't "just Google it"' on the InnerDrive Blog, 3 May. Available at: www. innerdrive.co.uk/blog/cant-just-google-it/ (accessed 16/10/25).

10 Puttick, H. (2023) 'What went wrong with the Scottish education system?' in *The Sunday Times*, 26 December. Available at: www. thetimes.com/uk/scotland/article/what-went-wrong-with-the-scottish-education-system-7qq8hbzlm?region=global (accessed 16/10/25).

11 Davies, K. and Henderson, P. (2025) *Special educational needs in mainstream schools: Guidance report*. London: Education Endowment Foundation. Available at: https://educationendowmentfoundation. org.uk/education-evidence/guidance-reports/send (accessed 16/10/25).

12 Scottish Government (2023) *Programme for International Student Assessment (PISA 2022): Highlights from Scotland's results*. Available at: www.gov.scot/publications/programme-international-student-assessment-pisa-2022-highlights-scotlands-results/ (accessed 16/10/25).

13 Ingram, J. *et al* (2023) *PISA 2022: National Report for England, Research report*. London: Department for Education and Oxford University. Available at: www.gov.uk/government/publications/pisa-2022-national-report-for-england (accessed 16/10/25).

Building a strong knowledge-rich curriculum: What does a well-sequenced knowledge-rich primary curriculum look like? *Emma Lennard*

1 Department for Education (2013) *The national curriculum in England: Key stages 1 and 2 framework document*. Available at: www.gov. uk/government/publications/national-curriculum-in-england-primary-curriculum (accessed 16/10/25).

2 Ausubel, D. P. (1968) *Educational Psychology: A Cognitive View*. New York: Holt, Rinehart & Winston.

3 Hattie, J. and Yates, G. (2013) *Visible Learning and the Science of How We Learn*. London: Routledge.

4 Department for Education (2013) *The national curriculum in England: Key stages 1 and 2 framework document*. Available at: www.gov. uk/government/publications/national-curriculum-in-england-primary-curriculum (accessed 16/10/25).

5 Didau, D. and Rose, N. (2016) *What every teacher needs to know about psychology*, p40. Woodbridge: John Catt Educational Limited.

Phonics and a knowledge-rich approach: Developing a phonics programme that delivers vocabulary and language knowledge alongside code knowledge, *Tara Dodson*

1 Essential Letters and Sounds (ELS), Oxford University Press. Available at: https://home.oxfordowl.co.uk/reading/reading-schemes-oxford-levels/essential-letters-and-sounds/ (accessed 16/10/25).

2 There are 17 early learning goals for children in the early years foundation stage statutory framework: they encompass communication and language; personal social and emotional development; physical development; literacy; mathematics; understanding the world; and expressive arts and design. The goals are assessed in the final term of reception year in primary school.

3 Department for Education (2014) *'Evidence check' memorandum: Phonics policy.* Available at: www.parliament.uk/globalassets/documents/commons-committees/Education/evidence-check-forum/phonics.pdf (accessed 16/10/25).

4 Rose, J. (2006) *Independent review of the teaching of early reading.* London: Department for Education and Skills. Available at: https://dera.ioe.ac.uk/id/eprint/5551/2/report.pdf (accessed 16/10/25).

5 Department for Education (2021) *The reading framework: Guidance for primary and secondary schools to meet existing expectations for teaching reading.* Available at: www.gov.uk/government/publications/the-reading-framework-teaching-the-foundations-of-literacy (accessed 16/10/25).

6 Owston, L. (2023) 'Pupils with special educational needs and/or disabilities who have fallen behind with reading' on the Ofsted Blog, 2 March. Available at: https://educationinspection.blog.gov.uk/2023/03/02/pupils-with-special-educational-needs-and-or-disabilities-who-have-fallen-behind-with-reading/ (accessed 16/10/25).

7 Sweller, J. (1988) 'Cognitive Load During Problem Solving: Effects on Learning' in *Cognitive Science*, 1988;12(2):257–285. Available at: https://onlinelibrary.wiley.com/doi/abs/10.1207/s15516709cog1202_4 (accessed 16/10/25).

8 Quigley, A. (2019) 'What do we mean by "knowledge rich" anyway?' on the Education Endowment Foundation Blog, 9 January. Available at: https://educationendowmentfoundation.org.uk/news/eef-blog-what-do-we-mean-by-knowledge-rich-anyway (accessed 16/10/25).

9   An orthographic map is the recognition that within a word the sound-to-spelling correspondences are concrete. For example, in 'bread' the <ea> is spelling the sound /e/ and you recognise this automatically every time you read the word. This is developed by repeated exposure to the word to allow this fluent recognition.

10   Gough, P. and Tunmer, W. (1986) 'Decoding, Reading, and Reading Disability' in *Remedial and Special Education*, 1986;7(1):6–10. Available at: https://doi.org/10.1177/074193258600700104 (accessed 16/10/25).

11   Kartushina, N. *et al* (2022) 'COVID-19 first lockdown as a window into language acquisition: associations between caregiver-child activities and vocabulary gains' in *Language Development Research*, 2022;2(1):1–36. Available at: https://shs.hal.science/halshs-03814773/file/Kartushina_etal_2022_COVID-19%20first%20lockdown%20as%20a%20window%20into%20language%20acquisition.pdf (accessed 16/10/25).

12   Ofsted (2024) *Strong foundations in the first years of school.* Available at: www.gov.uk/government/publications/strong-foundations-in-the-first-years-of-school/strong-foundations-in-the-first-years-of-school#a-clear-curriculum (accessed 16/10/25).

13   Barnes, E. and Puccioni, J. (2017) 'Shared book reading and preschool children's academic achievement: Evidence from the Early Childhood Longitudinal Study – Birth cohort' in *Infant and Child Development*, 2017;26(6):1–19. Available at: https://doi.org/10.1002/icd.2035 (accessed 16/10/25).

14   Niklas, F. *et al* (2016) 'Parents supporting learning: a non-intensive intervention supporting literacy and numeracy in the home learning environment' in *International Journal of Early Years Education*, 2016;24(2):121–142. Available at: https://doi.org/10.1080/09669760.2016.1155147 (accessed 16/10/25).

15   Golinkoff, R. M. *et al* (2018) 'Language Matters: Denying the Existence of the 30-Million-Word Gap Has Serious Consequences' in *Child Development*, 2018;90(3):985–992. Available at: https://srcd.onlinelibrary.wiley.com/doi/10.1111/cdev.13128 (accessed 16/10/25).

16   Quigley, A. (2019) 'What do we mean by "knowledge rich" anyway?' on the Education Endowment Foundation Blog, 9 January. Available at: https://educationendowmentfoundation.org.uk/news/eef-blog-what-do-we-mean-by-knowledge-rich-anyway (accessed 16/10/25).

A knowledge-rich approach to art: A primary school case study,
Naomi Pilling

1 Ofsted (2023) *Research review series: art and design*. Available at: www.gov.uk/government/publications/research-review-series-art-and-design/research-review-series-art-and-design (accessed 16/10/25).

2 Neuman, S. B. *et al* (2014) 'Building background knowledge' in *The Reading Teacher*, 2014;68(2):145–148.

3 Vonnegut, K. (2005) *A Man Without a Country*. New York: Seven Stories Press.

4 Young, M. *et al* (2014) *Knowledge and the Future School: Curriculum and Social Justice*. London: Bloomsbury Publishing.

5 Department for Education (2013) *Art and design programmes of study: key stages 1 and 2, National curriculum in England*. Available at: www.gov.uk/government/publications/national-curriculum-in-england-art-and-design-programmes-of-study (accessed 16/10/25).

6 Ofsted (2023) *Research review series: art and design*. Available at: www.gov.uk/government/publications/research-review-series-art-and-design/research-review-series-art-and-design (accessed 16/10/25).

7 Art UK, 'The Superpower of Looking'. Available at: https://artuk.org/learn/the-superpower-of-looking (accessed 16/10/25).

8 Tate, 'A guide to slow looking'. Available at: www.tate.org.uk/art/guide-slow-looking (accessed 16/10/25).

Knowledge for all, *Ben Newmark*

1 Lough, C. (2020) 'Dylan Wiliam: "Immoral" to teach "too full" curriculum' in *Tes magazine*, 28 April. Available at: www.tes.com/magazine/archive/dylan-wiliam-immoral-teach-too-full-curriculum (accessed 16/10/25).

2 Department for Education (2025) *Academic year 2023/24: Key stage 2 attainment*. Available at: https://explore-education-statistics.service.gov.uk/find-statistics/key-stage-2-attainment/2023-24 (accessed 16/10/25).

3 Rosenshine, B. (2012) 'Principles of Instruction: Research-Based Strategies That All Teachers Should Know' in *American Educator* 2012;36(1):12–39. Available at: www.aft.org/ae/spring2012 (accessed 16/10/25).

4 Lough, C. (2020) 'Dylan Wiliam: "Immoral" to teach "too full" curriculum' in *Tes magazine*, 28 April. Available at: www.tes.com/magazine/archive/dylan-wiliam-immoral-teach-too-full-curriculum (accessed 16/10/25).

5   de Tocqueville, A. (1835) *Democracy in America*, London: Saunders and Otley; and Mill, J. S. (1859) *On Liberty*, London: John W. Parker & Son.

From theory to practice: Implementing a knowledge-based secondary school curriculum for social equity, *Jeremy Baker*

1   For example, Young, M. *et al* (2014) *Knowledge and the Future School: Curriculum and Social Justice.* London: Bloomsbury Publishing; and Hirsch Jr., E. D. (1987) *Cultural Literacy: What Every American Needs to Know.* Boston, MA: Houghton Mifflin Harcourt Company.

2   Arnold, M. (1869) *Culture and Anarchy: An Essay in Political and Social Criticism.* London: Smith, Elder and Co.

3   Boxer, A. (ed) (2019) *The researchED Guide to Explicit & Direct Instruction: An evidence-informed guide for teachers.* Woodbridge: John Catt Educational Limited.

4   Furst, E. (2018) 'From neuroscience to the classroom' on researchED, 26 September. Available at: https://researched.org.uk/2018/09/26/from-neuroscience-to-the-classroom-2/ (accessed 16/10/25).

5   Ofsted (2021) *Curriculum research reviews: Subject reports.* Available at: www.gov.uk/government/collections/curriculum-research-reviews (accessed 16/10/25).

6   Young, M. *et al* (2014) *Knowledge and the Future School: Curriculum and Social Justice.* London: Bloomsbury Publishing.

7   Sharples, J. *et al* (2024) *A School's Guide to Implementation.* London: Education Endowment Foundation. Available at: https://d2tic4wvo1iusb.cloudfront.net/production/eef-guidance-reports/implementation/a_schools_guide_to_implementation.pdf?v=1753106580 (accessed 16/10/25).

Teaching a knowledge-rich secondary history curriculum, *Harry Hudson*

1   Dickens, C. (1854) 'Hard Times' in *Household Words*, 1854;9(210):141–145.

Implementing a knowledge-rich curriculum in a special needs school, *Kasia Glinka and Rebecca Ryman*

1   Ofsted (2019) *Education inspection framework: overview of research.* Available at: www.gov.uk/government/publications/education-inspection-framework-overview-of-research (accessed 16/10/25).

2   Ofsted (2021) *Curriculum research reviews: Subject reports.* Available at: www.gov.uk/government/collections/curriculum-research-reviews (accessed 16/10/25).

3 Labour's Council of Skills Advisors (2022) *Learning and skills for economic recovery, social cohesion and a more equal Britain*. Available at: https://labour.org.uk/wp-content/uploads/2022/10/WR-16813_22-Labour-Skills-Council-report-Edit-19-10-22.pdf (accessed 16/10/25).

4 Freire, P. (1970) *Pedagogy of the Oppressed*. New York: Seabury Press.

5 Ibid.

6 Willingham, D. (2006) 'Ask the Cognitive Scientist: The usefulness of *brief* instruction in reading comprehension strategies' in *American Educator*, 2006;30(4):39–50. Available at: www.aft.org/ae/winter2006-2007/willingham (accessed 16/10/25).

7 Young, M. and Muller, J. (2013) 'On the powers of powerful knowledge' in *Review of Education*, 2013;1(3):229–250. Available at: https://bera-journals.onlinelibrary.wiley.com/doi/abs/10.1002/rev3.3017 (accessed 16/10/25).

Intellectual discipline: A knowledge-rich behaviour curriculum,
Tom Bennett
1 Department for Education (2024) *Behaviour in Schools: Advice for headteachers and school staff*. Available at: https://assets.publishing.service.gov.uk/media/65ce3721e1bdec001a3221fe/Behaviour_in_schools_-_advice_for_headteachers_and_school_staff_Feb_2024.pdf (accessed 22/10/25).

The role of knowledge in the school curriculum: A US case study,
David Steiner
1 Recht, D. R. and Leslie, L. (1988) 'Effect of prior knowledge on good and poor readers' memory of text' in *Journal of Educational Psychology*, 1988;80(1):16–20. Available at: www.researchgate.net/publication/232584848_Effect_of_Prior_Knowledge_on_Good_and_Poor_Readers'_Memory_of_Text (accessed 16/10/25).

2 Hirsch Jr., E. D. (2016) *Why Knowledge Matters: Rescuing our Children from Failed Educational Theories*. Cambridge, MA: Harvard Education Press.

3 Ibid.

4 Oates, T. (2021) 'England: England and PISA – The Long View' in Crato, N. (ed) *Improving a Country's Education: PISA 2018 Results in 10 Countries*. Cham, Switzerland: Springer. Available at: https://link.springer.com/book/10.1007/978-3-030-59031-4 (accessed 16/10/25).

5   Kirp, D. L. (2015) *Improbable Scholars: The Rebirth of a Great American School System and a Strategy for America's Schools*. Reprint edition. Oxford: Oxford University Press.

6   *McGuffey's Eclectic Readers:* www.britannica.com/topic/McGuffey-Readers (accessed 16/10/25).

7   US Census Bureau (2024) *School Districts and Associated Counties: Districts and Counties by Year*. Available at: www.census.gov/programs-surveys/saipe/guidance-geographies/districts-counties.html (accessed 16/10/25).

8   TNTP (2018) *The Opportunity Myth: What Students Can Show Us About How School Is Letting Them Down – and How to Fix It*. Available at: https://tntp.org/publication/the-opportunity-myth/ (accessed 16/10/25).

9   Ibid.

10 Chambers, J. (2025) 'Students in poverty more likely to have inexperienced teachers, report says' on EdTrust-Midwest, 14 January. Available at: https://midwest.edtrust.org/news/students-in-poverty-more-likely-to-have-inexperienced-teachers-report-says/ (accessed 16/10/25).

11 National Assessment Governing Board (2025) *10 Takeaways from the 2024 NAEP Results*. Available at: www.nagb.gov/powered-by-naep/the-2024-nations-report-card/10-takeaways-from-2024-naep-results.html (accessed 16/10/25).

12 Kaufman, J. H. *et al* (2017) *Use of Open Educational Resources in an Era of Common Standards: A Case Study on the Use of EngageNY*. Santa Monica, CA: RAND Corporation. Available at: www.rand.org/content/dam/rand/pubs/research_reports/RR1700/RR1773/RAND_RR1773.pdf (accessed 16/10/25).

13 National Center for Education Statistics (2025) *State and Urban Districts Snapshots* (2024 data). Washington, DC: The Institute of Education Sciences. Available at: https://nces.ed.gov/nationsreportcard/snapshots/ (accessed 16/10/25).

14 Kane, T. *et al* (2019) *Learning by the Book: Comparing math achievement growth by textbook in six Common Core states*. Cambridge, MA: Center for Education Policy Research, Harvard University. Available at: https://cepr.harvard.edu/curriculum (accessed 16/10/25).

15 Steiner, D. (2024) 'Why Teachers Don't Use the High-Quality Instructional Materials They're Given' on The74, 12 November. Available at: www.the74million.org/article/why-teachers-dont-use-the-high-quality-instructional-materials-theyre-given/ (accessed 16/10/25).

16   Ibid.

17   The Achievement Network (ANet): www.achievementnetwork.org/
     about-us (accessed 16/10/25).

18   Modern Classrooms Project: www.modernclassrooms.org/
     (accessed 16/10/25).

The fragility of knowledge in England's schools, *Christine Counsell*

1   See Chapter 2 of Hirsch Jr., E. D. (1988) *Cultural Literacy: What Every
     American Needs to Know.* New York: Vintage.

2   Willingham, D. (2017) *The Reading Mind: A Cognitive Approach to
     Understanding How the Mind Reads.* San Francisco, CA: Jossey-Bass.

3   Young, M. (2007) *Bringing Knowledge Back In: From social
     constructivism to social realism in the sociology of education.* London:
     Routledge.

4   Young, M. *et al* (2014) *Knowledge and the Future School: Curriculum
     and Social Justice.* London: Bloomsbury Publishing.

5   For example, Healy, G. (2021) 'A Call to View Disciplinary
     Knowledge Through the Lens of Geography Teachers' Professional
     Practice' in Fargher, M. *et al* (eds) (2021) *Recontextualising Geography
     in Education*, pp71–88. Cham, Switzerland: Springer. Available at:
     https://link.springer.com/chapter/10.1007/978-3-030-73722-1_6
     (accessed 16/11/25).

6   Fordham, M. (2016) 'Realising and extending Stenhouse's vision
     of teacher research: The case of English history teachers' in *British
     Educational Research Journal*, 2016;42(1):135–150.

7   Counsell, C. (2011) 'Disciplinary knowledge for all, the secondary
     history curriculum and history teachers' achievement' in *The
     Curriculum Journal*, 2011;22(2):201–225. Available at: https://bera-
     journals.onlinelibrary.wiley.com/doi/abs/10.1080/09585176.2011.57
     4951 (accessed 16/11/25).

8   For example, Hammond, K. (2014) 'The knowledge that "flavours" a
     claim: towards building and assessing historical knowledge on three
     scales' in *Teaching History*, 2014;157:18–24. Available at: www.history.
     org.uk/publications/resource/8133/building-and-assessing-
     historical-knowledge-on-thr (accessed 16/11/25).

9   Koretz, D. (2008) *Measuring Up: What Educational Testing Really Tells
     Us.* Cambridge, MA: Harvard University Press.

10   Christodoulou, D. (2016) *Making Good Progress? The future of
     Assessment for Learning.* Oxford: Oxford University Press.

11   Such, C. (2021) *The Art and Science of Teaching Primary Reading.*
     London: Sage Publications.

12 Hirsch Jr., E. D. (1988) *Cultural Literacy: What Every American Needs to Know*. New York: Vintage.

13 Fordham, M. (2020) 'What did I mean by "the curriculum is the progression model"?' on Clio et cetera, 8 February. Available at: https://clioetcetera.com/2020/02/08/what-did-i-mean-by-the-curriculum-is-the-progression-model/ (accessed 16/11/25).

14 Department for Education (2024) *Initial Teacher Training and Early Career Framework*. Available at: www.gov.uk/government/publications/initial-teacher-training-and-early-career-framework (accessed 16/11/25).

15 Rosenshine, B. (2012) 'Principles of Instruction: Research-Based Strategies That All Teachers Should Know' in *American Educator*, 2012;36(1):12–39. Available at: www.aft.org/ae/spring2012 (accessed 16/11/25).

16 Ofsted (2019) *Education inspection framework (EIF)*. Available at: www.gov.uk/government/publications/education-inspection-framework (accessed 16/11/25).

17 Ofsted (2018) 'HMCI commentary: curriculum and the new education inspection framework' on Gov.uk, 18 September. Available at: www.gov.uk/government/speeches/hmci-commentary-curriculum-and-the-new-education-inspection-framework (accessed 16/11/25).

18 The 2019 EIF was replaced in October 2025, and subject curriculum quality became much less central. Ofsted's curriculum unit, set up by Spielman to provide subject reviews and subject-specific training for inspectors, was phased out after Spielman's term finished.

19 Ofsted (2023) *Subject report series: history*. Available at: www.gov.uk/government/publications/subject-report-series-history (accessed 16/11/25).

20 Such, C. (2021) *The Art and Science of Teaching Primary Reading*. London: Sage Publications.

21 Counsell, C. (2023) 'Laughing muppets, lost memories and lethal mutations: rescuing assessment from "knowledge-rich gone wrong"' in *Teaching History*, 2023;193:8–25. Available at: www.history.org.uk/publications/resource/10825/rescuing-assessment-from-knowledge-rich-gone-wrong (accessed 16/11/25).

22 This argument is further developed in Counsell, C. and Healy, G. (2025) 'Challenging genericism: what is at stake for curriculum and teacher development?' in Barrett, B. *et al* (eds) *Knowledge Production, Policy and Practice in Education: Social realist explorations of curriculum, teaching and research*. London: Routledge.

23 See the Historical Association (2020) 'What's the wisdom on…
    enquiry questions' in *Teaching History*, 2020;178:16–19. Available
    at: www.history.org.uk/publications/resource/9778/whats-the-
    wisdom-on-enquiry-questions?srsltid=AfmBOooBezw5KmoHCTior
    rfvEpHA-EgeQ9w3aEsN59HlTfmurM-U3X-L (accessed 16/11/25).

24 Pickles, E. (2011) 'Assessment of students' uses of evidence: Shifting
    the focus from processes to historical reasoning' in *Teaching History*,
    2011;143:52–59. Available at: www.history.org.uk/publications/
    resource/4656/assessment-of-students-uses-of-evidence?srs
    ltid=AfmBOop7pJfgcd09u8BzHA12RwOHhI5WM-3Jd-fCn_
    P7ODLzCMBU6LD3 (accessed 16/11/25).

25 Further examples of 'knowledge-rich gone wrong' can be found
    in Counsell, C. (2023) 'Laughing muppets, lost memories and
    lethal mutations: rescuing assessment from "knowledge-rich gone
    wrong"' in *Teaching History*, 2023;193:8–25. Available at: www.
    history.org.uk/publications/resource/10825/rescuing-assessment-
    from-knowledge-rich-gone-wrong (accessed 16/11/25).

26 Counsell, C. (2016) 'Genericism's children' on The Dignity of the
    Thing, 11 January. Available at: https://thedignityofthethingblog.
    wordpress.com/2016/01/11/genericisms-children/ (accessed
    16/11/25).

27 I have discussed the continuing relevance of Genericism's children
    on the podcast 'They Behave For Me'. Available at: https://open.
    spotify.com/episode/4UZrevypDHe6p83snOzgmC (accessed
    16/11/25).

28 Department for Education (2020) *National Professional Qualification
    (NPQ): Senior Leadership Framework*. Available at: https://assets.
    publishing.service.gov.uk/media/63a1dc7a8fa8f539198d9bca/
    NPQ_Senior_Leadership_FINAL_Ref.pdf (accessed 16/11/25).

29 Such questions are exemplified in Counsell, C. (2020) 'Better
    conversations with subject leaders: How secondary senior leaders
    can see a curriculum more clearly' in Sealy, C. (ed) (2020) *The
    researchED Guide to the Curriculum*, pp95–121. Woodbridge: John
    Catt Educational Limited.

30 Readers who are unaware of the serious decline in reading whole
    novels might read this wake-up call by Carl Hendrick: Hendrick,
    C. (2025) 'In Defence of the Whole: Why Students Should Read
    Books Not Just Extracts' on The Learning Dispatch, 15 November.
    Available at: https://carlhendrick.substack.com/p/in-defence-of-
    the-whole-why-students (accessed 16/11/25).

31 Maton, K. (2014) *Knowledge and Knowers: Towards a realist sociology of education*. London: Routledge.

32 For a fuller account of the disciplinary dimension of school subjects, see Counsell, C. (2018) 'Taking curriculum seriously' in *Impact*, Issue 4, Chartered College of Teaching. Available at: https://my.chartered.college/impact_article/taking-curriculum-seriously/ (accessed 16/11/25).

33 Counsell, C. and Healy, G. (2025) 'Challenging genericism: what is at stake for curriculum and teacher development?' in Barrett, B. *et al* (eds) *Knowledge Production, Policy and Practice in Education: Social realist explorations of curriculum, teaching and research*. London: Routledge.

CIVITAS

Our Aims and Programmes
- We facilitate informed public debate by providing accurate factual information on the social issues of the day, publishing informed comment and analysis, and bringing together leading protagonists in open discussion. Civitas never takes a corporate view on any of the issues tackled during the course of this work. Our current focus is on issues such as education, health, crime, social security, manufacturing, the abuse of human rights law, and the European Union.

- We ensure that there is strong evidence for all our conclusions and present the evidence in a balanced and objective way. Our publications are usually refereed by independent commentators, who may be academics or experts in their field.

- We strive to benefit public debate through independent research, reasoned argument, lucid explanation and open discussion. We stand apart from party politics and transitory intellectual fashions.

- Uniquely among think tanks, we play an active, practical part in rebuilding civil society by running schools on Saturdays and after-school hours so that children who are falling behind at school can achieve their full potential.

Subscriptions and Membership (UK only)
If you would like to stay abreast of Civitas' latest work, you can have all of our books delivered to your door as soon as they are published. New subscribers receive a free copy of Roger Bootle's book, *The AI Economy: Work, Wealth and Welfare in the Robot Age* and Daniel Bentley's book, *The Land Question* on fixing the dysfunction at the root of the housing crisis. For those who would like to support our work further and get involved in our Westminster events, we have a variety of Subscription and Membership options available:
https://www.civitasonline.org.uk/product-category/subscriptions/

We regret that we are unable to post items to non-UK residents, although all of our publications are individually available via our Civitas Book Store (https://www.civitasonline.org.uk) and in most cases on Amazon.

Renewals for Existing Members

If you are an existing member wishing to renew with ease and convenience, please do select one of the subscription or membership options that most closely meets your requirements.

Make a Donation

If you like our work and would like to help see it continue, please consider making a donation. A contribution of any amount, big or small, will help us advance our research and educational activities. You can make a donation by getting in touch (020 7799 6677) or sending a simple email to info@civitas.org.uk so that we can come back to you.

Supporters of Civitas

Because we want to reach as wide an audience as possible, our subscription and membership fees are set as low as possible and barely meet printing and postage expenses. To meet the costs of producing our research and conducting our educational projects, we rely entirely on the goodwill and generosity of people who value our work.

If you would like to support our work on a rolling basis, there is a variety of advanced membership levels on offer. Supporters of Civitas have the opportunity to become more deeply engaged with the work their philanthropy makes possible.

You can pay by selecting a membership or subscription option and we will be in contact.

Alternatively, just call us on +44 (0)20 7799 6677
or email info@civitas.org.uk and we can discuss your options.

If it is your preference, please make cheques payable to Civitas.

Civitas: Institute for the Study of Civil Society
First Floor
55 Tufton Street
Westminster
London
SW1P 3QL

Email: subs@civitas.org.uk